EDWIN LUTYENS
COUNTRY HOUSES

EDWIN LUTYENS
COUNTRY HOUSES

FROM THE ARCHIVES OF COUNTRY LIFE

GAVIN STAMP

For
Cecilia Jane Stamp

First published in Great Britain 2001 by Aurum Press Limited
7 Greenland Street, London NW1 0ND
www.aurumpress.co.uk

This paperback edition first published in 2012 by Aurum Press

A catalogue record for this book is available from the British Library

ISBN 978 1 84513 765 6

1 3 5 7 9 10 8 6 4 2

2012 2014 2016 2018 2017 2015 2013

Design by James Campus
Series Editor: Michael Hall

Originated by Colorlito-CST S.r.l., Milan
Printed and bound in China

Frontispiece: *Deanery Garden, the house Lutyens designed for Edward Hudson,*
the founder of Country Life, *in 1899; photograph by Charles Latham, first published in 1903.*

THE COUNTRY LIFE PICTURE LIBRARY

The *Country Life* Picture Library holds a complete set of prints
made from its negatives, and a card index to the subjects, usually
recording the name of the photographer and the date of the
photographs catalogued, together with a separate index of
photographers. It also holds a complete set of *Country Life* and
various forms of published indices to the magazine. The Library
may be visited by appointment, and prints of any negatives it
holds can be supplied by post.

For further information, please contact the Library Manager,
Justin Hobson, at *Country Life*, Blue Fin Building,
110 Southwark Street, London SE1 0SU (*Tel:* 020 3148 4474).

ACKNOWLEDGEMENTS

I am deeply grateful to Michael Hall, the series editor and
deputy editor of *Country Life*, for giving me the opportunity to
write this book and so to indulge in reviving the old enthusiasms
by which I had been much consumed at the time of the great
Lutyens Exhibition at the Hayward Gallery in 1981–82. In
writing the text, I have benefited from conversations with and/or
writings by the several colleagues involved in the happy project
of organising that exhibition, notably Colin Amery, Jane Brown,
Peter Inskip, Margaret Richardson and the late Roderick
Gradidge, who did so much to revive Lutyens's reputation.
I have also made extensive use of the correspondence between
Lutyens and his wife, the former Lady Emily Lytton, published
by the architect's great-granddaughter, Jane Ridley, and her
mother, Clayre Percy. Jane Ridley has also assisted me in this
project and I hope that her new biography of Lutyens together
with this book may reflect a new interest in an extraordinary
man and the greatest British architect of the last century.

I should also like to acknowledge the help and advice given
me by (as well as, again, the writings by) John Cornforth,
particularly with regard to Lutyens's relationship with *Country
Life* and the magazine's authors and photographers. As for the
photographs themselves, the compilation here could not have
been made without the advice and assistance of Camilla Costello,
librarian at the *Country Life* Picture Library, helped by Olive
Waller. I am also grateful to Rosemary Hill for reading the
text and offering useful advice. I only wish I could have
discussed this book with the late Mary Lutyens and given
her a copy.

The portrait of Sir Edwin Lutyens on *page* 10 is reproduced
by courtesy of the Art Workers Guild Trustees Ltd, London /
Bridgeman Art Library.

CONTENTS

I N a particular view of England, *Country Life*, country life and the houses designed by Edwin Lutyens may seem inseparable. The magazine and its book-publishing arm certainly did the architect proud. *The Life of Sir Edwin Lutyens* by Christopher Hussey was first published by *Country Life* in 1950 and it remains the finest biography of an architect in the English language. 'The genius of Lutyens,' Hussey began, 'was a legend that dawned on the early Edwardians, had become a portent before the First World War, and remained a fixed star in the architectural firmament, despite the rising of the constellation of Le Corbusier, until his death on New Year's Day 1944 ... . In his lifetime he was widely held to be our greatest architect since Wren if not, as many maintained, his superior.'[1]

Hussey's *Life*, together with the three accompanying folio volumes of drawings and photographs by A. S. G. Butler, constituted the *Lutyens Memorial*. All were published by *Country Life* (in association with Charles Scribner's Sons of New York) and these magnificent books were the apotheosis of half a century of illustrating and promoting Lutyens's architecture by the company since Crooksbury, his first house, had appeared in the pages of the magazine in 1900. There was a symbiotic relationship between architect and publisher, and Lutyens designed the headquarters of *Country Life* in Covent Garden in 1904. That building, a subtle homage to Lutyens's greatest hero, Sir Christopher Wren, is, alas, no longer occupied by the magazine; the legacy that remains, however, is the superb collection of images of Lutyens's buildings taken by *Country Life*'s photographers during his lifetime and beyond. Hence this book.

When the *Lutyens Memorial* appeared half a century ago, its subject was beginning to seem problematic. As an upholder of tradition and of the value of the Classical language of architecture, and as an expensive architect of expensive country houses, Lutyens's achievement was seen as an irrelevance by a younger generation of architects inspired by the Modern Movement and by the ideal of a more egalitarian society. This was true even of his own architect son, Robert, who later recalled that he 'found Andrew Butler's text in the Memorial Volumes of such a boredom that I, at least, fell into the error of supposing that the work itself was boring – a period product of only passing significance – to be glanced at in some splendid photographs and put away.'[2] Reviews of these books were respectful, but somehow distant; their subject was now seen as an historical phenomenon, not – as the authors had hoped – as a model and inspiration for the future.

The most intriguing tribute to Lutyens, because unexpected, came from another great architect on the other side of the Atlantic. In reviewing the books in *Building* magazine in 1951, Frank Lloyd Wright was pleased to

Great Maytham, rebuilt by Lutyens in 1907–09 and one of his largest essays in his 'Wrennaissance' manner, seen from the road through the stables.

voice admiration of the love, loyalty and art with which this cultured architect, in love with Architecture, shaped his buildings. To him the English chimney, the Gable, the Gatepost monumentalized in good brickwork and cut-stone were motifs to be dramatized with great skill. He was able to idealize them with a success unequalled. Nor can I think of anyone able to so characteristically and quietly dramatize the old English feeling for dignity and comfort in an interior, however or wherever that interior might be in England.[3]

Wright was Lutyens's near contemporary. They began their careers at about the same time by designing houses and, in the 1890s, they had much in common. In fact, the three close contemporaries, Frank Lloyd Wright, Charles Rennie Mackintosh and Edwin Landseer Lutyens, born in the three successive years 1867, 1868 and 1869 respectively, became the most interesting architects practising in the English-speaking world at the beginning of the twentieth century, and significant connections and parallels may be drawn between them in their work. Later, their careers diverged and while Wright carried on, ever inventive, until his death in harness in 1959, Mackintosh effectively gave up architecture when he left Glasgow in 1914. (Lutyens's later, inventive and abstracted Classical work may also be usefully compared with the designs of the great Slovenian architect, Joze Plečnik, born in 1872, but that is another story.)

Lutyens, like Wright but unlike Mackintosh, changed direction and continually developed. Anxious to tackle a 'big job', he moved on from the vernacular of his native Surrey to engage with the grammar and discipline of Renaissance Classicism – the language of Palladio, Sanmicheli, and Wren – and became increasingly preoccupied with geometry and proportion. He became the architect of New Delhi, the new capital of British India, and one of the principal architects to – and the principal artistic influence on – the Imperial War Graves Commission, for which he designed some of his most abstract, austere and moving works such as the Memorial to the Missing of the Somme at Thiepval in France, arguably the greatest British monument of the last century. Knighted in 1918, he went on to design banks and commercial offices, and, finally, what would have been his supreme achievement had it been completed: Liverpool Metropolitan Cathedral. Although part of the crypt was realised, this was a work which, as Robert Lutyens later wrote, now stands 'quite outside time and period ... . It may well have been the final affirmation of his faith in the eternal thing that so transcends mere building. It is architecture – asserted once and for ever – and the very greatest building that was never built!'[4]

When Lutyens died, surrounded by drawings of his cathedral, on New Year's Day, 1944, in the dark days of the Second World War, it was felt that not only had a great man departed but that an era had ended. 'Lutyens absent, the architectural scene is colder,' concluded the obituary in the *Architect and Building News*. 'December fog shrouds the façades of Britannic House, as it has covered already the Corinthian epics of Cooper, Blomfield's sturdy Doric, and all the old grey and black of Victorian London. A whole age has receded and its last monarch, Lutyens the magnificent, has resigned the sceptre.'[5]

'He was a magician, a spell-binder, and few of us have not been in thrall to him,' wrote H. S. Goodhart-Rendel. 'He seems to leave behind him a grey world, full of grim architectural Puritans on the one hand and gentleman-like architects who do the done thing on the other. He took Shaw's place, but who is to take his?'[6] Such was the stature of the late Sir Edwin Lutyens, OM, PRA.

Yet, had Lutyens died forty years earlier in, say, 1904, he would still be remembered today as the most brilliant designer of houses of his generation: houses in which the vernacular manner adopted by Philip Webb and Norman Shaw in the previous century was developed with originality and wit and with remarkable formal control. This is the aspect of his achievement which, on the whole, has most interested recent critics and historians. In 1904, the Prussian architect Hermann Muthesius published (in German, and in Berlin) his perceptive and thorough study of *Das englische Haus* and noted that Lutyens

is a young man who of recent years has come increasingly to the forefront of domestic architects and who may soon become the accepted leader among English builders of houses, like Norman Shaw in the past. Lutyens is one of those architects who would refuse to have anything whatever to do with any new movement ... . But just as a really important artist cannot ignore the demands of his time, so Lutyens's new buildings do not really look ancient at all. On the contrary, they have a character that, if not modern, is entirely personal and extremely interesting.[7]

The work by Lutyens that Muthesius chose to illustrate was Orchards, near Godalming, but he also included a plan of the gardens at Deanery Garden at Sonning, the house commissioned in 1899 by Edward Hudson (1854–1936), the founder and proprietor of *Country Life*. This was not only one of Lutyens's finest houses – a design in which the integration of interior and exterior space around dominant axes can very usefully be compared with contemporary 'prairie houses' by Wright – but the tangible beginning of an association between architect and publisher. 'There is no parallel in architectural publishing to *Country Life*'s championship of Edwin Lutyens,' John Cornforth has written, 'and even now it is hard to see his buildings uninfluenced by the distinctive eye of *Country Life* photographs ...'.[8]

'Hudson possessed those indefinable qualities of an inspiring patron that enabled an artist to give of his best,' observes Cornforth. 'Moreover that was also to be part of the secret of his success as Editor of *Country Life*: he was able to get the best out of a remarkable company of contributors who remained loyal for many years. That is all the more remarkable, because he lacked grace and charm in his dealings with colleagues ...'.[9] He was not an easy man, and Lady Emily Lutyens did not care for him very much. Cornforth concludes that

Hudson, although a kind man, does not seem to have been an entertaining or stimulating companion like Lutyens. That makes me feel that one great bond between them was what could be done with *Country Life* and it was

that interest that was crucial to the continuity of their friendship ... . Hudson's inarticulate nature makes him a difficult figure to fathom, but he had appreciated talented people ... . As far as Hudson was concerned Lutyens was the greatest figure in his life, and what is striking is how wide ranging was his support for him.[10]

Hudson was both promoter and patron, and he would eventually commission two more houses from Lutyens – Lindisfarne Castle and Plumpton Place – in addition to alterations to his town house in Queen Anne's Gate. And then there was the new house for the magazine in Covent Garden, that conspicuous homage to Wren, exquisitely detailed and full of subtleties, with its tall chimneys which 'look enormous, like two campaniles perched on my big roof'. It was the ambitious architect's first important building in London. John Cornforth recalled that 'Lutyens's office was a stimulating background for seventy-two years and its loss undermined the editorial staff's sense of identification with the magazine. In many ways it was impractical, but it gave pleasure every day. From the outset it was intended to look like a slice of Hampton Court Palace, and the main editorial offices were on the *piano nobile*.'[11]

Hussey wrote of architect and patron that they 'had much in common in their natures. Both were largely self-educated, with an instinctive appreciation of beauty; both were inarticulate, Hudson finding his means of expression in his publications.' Hudson's personal patronage of Lutyens and his publication of his works was, Cornforth believes, 'balanced by a significant ... influence of the architect on the development of the style and approach of the

The former Country Life *building in Tavistock Street, Covent Garden, London (1904–05) designed on the theme of Wren at Hampton Court.*

The entrance front of Tigbourne Court, Witley, Surrey (1899–1901) as photographed when new for Country Life*: note the low height of the camera above the ground which helps to exaggerate the apparent size of the house.*

magazine'. The first Lutyens houses which appeared in its pages were photographed by Charles Latham and described by Gertrude Jekyll, who had introduced her protégé to the publisher. Her own house by Lutyens, Munstead Wood, was written up in 1900 (probably by E. Theodore Cook) and Hussey considered that the accompanying photographs by Latham, such as that of the first-floor gallery, 'can be recognised as marking a revolution in the presentation of interiors by its concentration on the spatial factor'.[12] Later, after 1907, Avray Tipping wrote the articles about Lutyens's houses but the most important author for Lutyens was Lawrence Weaver, who joined the staff of *Country Life* in 1909.

It was Weaver who compiled the book illustrating the *Houses and Gardens by E. L. Lutyens*, first published by *Country Life* in 1913, reprinted the following year and again in 1925. What the influential book published by Wasmuth in Berlin in 1911 was to Wright, this large and lavish production was to Lutyens. Sir Hubert Worthington, a former assistant, later recalled that 'The first

Country Life book was published at the end of my time in the office, and the whole of the aristocratic London world was at his feet. Clients continually came to the door, and the Aston Webb people were jealous – they were next door – when we had three more carriages than they had or when we had two noblemen and they had only two.'[13] (Sir Aston Webb, after all, was the architect of Buckingham Palace.)

In his preface, Weaver wrote that he had decided to present all of Lutyens's domestic work as a whole for the first time (for much of the material had already appeared in the pages of the magazine) as 'the moment seems appropriate'. He had just been elected an associate of the Royal Academy and appointed as architect for New Delhi, so 'the year 1913 sees him in some sort at a parting of the ways'. Lutyens did very well by Weaver and *Country Life*. The extent to which the architect influenced the view it presents must be speculation, but it is known that Hudson took a close interest in the way houses were recorded in *Country Life* articles and it is noticeable that with Lutyens's buildings (as with many of the early views of Wright's houses) the photographer chose a low viewpoint, thereby exaggerating the apparent size of the subject. The often-reproduced dramatic view of the entrance front of Tigbourne Court is a case in point. And the prints were sometimes retouched, eliminating, say, unsightly chimney pots above Lutyens's big stacks.

Not that Lutyens was completely satisfied (no architect ever is). 'My book by Weaver arrived today. It does make me hot,' he wrote to his wife from India. 'I do wish he had not mentioned Delhi so often and O dear it is just a catalogue of mistakes and failures. Clients who when I first started – I don't mean Chippy [Arthur Chapman] of course – did not know enough to direct and afterwards enough to lead. So fares the world. The only attainment possible nowadays seems to be words, words, words.'[14] But he had no cause to complain; as his author noted in his preface,

I could not have attempted this book if I had not a deep, but I trust not uncritical, admiration for what Sir Edwin has done and is doing. My only complaint is that he has hindered rather than helped me, by being very sparing of information and by refusing to read proofs. While this does honour to his modesty, it is somewhat disconcerting to a writer who attaches importance to accuracy of detail ...

Edwin Landseer Lutyens was born on 29 March 1869 in London, but he was partly brought up in Surrey. Ned, as he was always known, was the ninth son and tenth of the thirteen children of Captain Charles Henry Augustus Lutyens, a soldier and inventor turned painter (at which profession he was only initially successful) descended from Barthold Lütkens, who had moved from Hamburg to London during the reign of George II. Lutyens's mother was Mary Theresa Gallwey from Killarney, the daughter of a major in

Portrait of Sir Edwin Lutyens as Master of the Art Workers Guild in 1933 by Meredith Frampton.

the Royal Irish Constabulary. Captain Lutyens, whom she had met in Montreal, was a friend of Sir Edwin Landseer who, according to family legend, wanted to adopt the boy but she disapproved of the painter's morals. So the future architect was given his name instead. (And, as regards the pronunciation of his surname, 'the Lut rhymes with hut'.)

Lutyens's brothers all went to public school; Ned did not because he had rheumatic fever when young and was considered too delicate. He seems to have attended a day school in London, but only for two years. Sometimes Lutyens would express regret that he had not been better educated, as his friend and later rival, Herbert Baker, had been. But, in fact, he had the best possible education for an architect. 'Any talent I may have had,' he later told Osbert Sitwell, 'was due to a long illness as a boy, which afforded me time to think, and to subsequent ill-health, because I was not allowed to play games, and so had to teach myself, for my enjoyment, to use my eyes instead of my feet. My brothers hadn't the same advantage.'[15]

In 1876, Lutyens's mother took a substantial house called The Cottage at Thursley near Godalming as a second home and from then on the family spent half of their time in the country. Much of the quality of Lutyens's architecture was due to his experience of rural Surrey, for he would roam the countryside, looking at old buildings or new ones under construction, learning to use his eyes and his imagination. Sometimes he would visit the local village carpenter or go to the local builder's yard in Godalming to see men at work, thereby acquiring the knowledge of building materials and craftsmanship and awareness of the importance of detail that are so evident in his houses. This also enabled him to get on well with and win the respect of the craftsmen who built his buildings – a crucial aspect of the art of architecture that determines real quality. As Mary Lutyens wrote in her biography of her father,

He was intensely inquisitive about the few things that really interested him, and he had a remarkably quick eye and a phenomenal memory for detail ... . Ned as a boy devised his own means of teaching himself perspective and accuracy. He would carry about with him in his wanderings a small pane of clear glass and several pieces of soap sharpened to fine points. Looking through the glass at some detail of a building he wanted to learn about he would trace it with the soap.[16]

By such means, surely, did Lutyens develop his acute comprehension of three-dimensional form in terms of wall and roof planes.

A neighbour in Thursley was the artist Randolph Caldecott, who illustrated children's books with drawings of old farms, cottages and inns. It has often been suggested that such images of vernacular buildings inspired Ned Lutyens to become an architect, although his daughter disagreed:

I believe it is far more likely that he *had* to become an architect – one cannot think of any other art at which he would have excelled. It was the natural outcome of his talents for mathematics, drawing and observation, combined with his extraordinary visual memory. These gifts he may have inherited. That he also had a creative imagination of genius is one of those

Ruckmans, Oakwood Park (1894), was an old Surrey farm-house enlarged by Lutyens for the Misses Lyell.

genetic freaks that cannot be analysed or explained. Fortunately for him he had no great versatility, the curse of so many artists, and no real interests outside his creative work.

Possibly on the advice of Caldecott, Captain Lutyens enrolled his son at the National Art Training School in South Kensington in 1885. He did not finish the course, leaving after two years in the belief that he had learned all it had to teach him. By now Lutyens was determined to become a 'successful architect' and so, at the age of eighteen, he became an articled pupil in the office of Ernest George & Peto. Sir Ernest George was a prolific designer of picturesque country houses, usually Tudor in style, and the principal professional rival of the great Richard Norman Shaw (whose office Lutyens would rather have joined, but there was a long waiting list). Again, he stayed for only a year with George, about whose work and love of sketching he was later unfairly disparaging. In truth, he learned much in this lively and talented office – not least, as Margaret Richardson points out, how 'to design and draw in a pictorial manner', for George was a fine draughtsman and artist.[17] And it was here that he met his future collaborator Herbert Baker, with whom he would go on a sketching tour in Shropshire and Wales two years later. At the end of his life, Baker later recalled how his former friend, 'though joking through his short pupilage, quickly absorbed all that was best worth learning: he puzzled us at first, but we soon found that he seemed to know by intuition some great truths of our art which were not to be learned there'.[18]

Early in 1889, Lutyens set up on his own, having received a commission from Arthur Chapman, a family friend, to design Crooksbury, a small country house near Farnham in Surrey (this was not his first work, for he had enlarged The Corner at Thursley for Edmund Gray while still in George's office). Such a precocious start to a career is unthinkable today. However, the first portion of

Crooksbury and the houses that immediately followed are not particularly remarkable; the young architect had yet to develop a style of his own. 'All honour to Philip Webb and Norman Shaw ... for their gallant attempt to bring England back to craftsmanship and tradition,' he wrote, and in his early work Lutyens was building on that fashionable revival of the vernacular of the Home Counties which had seemed to be a satisfactory domestic alternative both to the Gothic and to the full-blown Classical. This was a manner of building, resonant with historical associations, which can be traced back to the cottages of John Nash but which really began to flourish in the mid-century in the work of George Devey and Anthony Salvin; thanks, in particular, to Shaw and his partner W. E. Nesfield, such domestic building had been at the cutting edge of architectural design since the 1860s.

Lutyens's early works certainly show the effect of the time he had spent with Ernest George; they also reflect the influence of Norman Shaw and Philip Webb. Webb was a particular hero, and Lutyens would publish a tribute to him – in *Country Life*, where else? – after his death in 1915. The lifelong friend of William Morris, whose house he had designed, Webb showed how it was possible to mix precedents creatively while building superbly. 'The freshness and originality which Webb maintained in all his work,' Lutyens recalled, 'I, in my ignorance, attributed to youth. I did not recognise it then to be the eternal youth of genius, though it was conjoined with another attribute of genius – thoroughness.'[19] Not that Lutyens was uncritical, maintaining that 'Had Webb started his career under the influence of Alfred Stevens rather than of Edmund Street, had he come into touch with those who could have bent his constructive genius to the grand manner of architecture, there would have been produced a man of astounding mark in the authentic line of Western architecture' – which is interesting, as Goodhart-Rendel later argued, unfashionably, that Lutyens's own work 'was the final flowering of the school of George Edmund Street', that great and original Victorian Goth.[20] Lutyens may first have become aware of Webb – and of Morris, the Society for the Protection of Ancient Buildings and other aspects of the Arts and Crafts movement – by meeting the young Detmar Blow, Ruskin's disciple, at South Kensington. Even so, Lutyens's architecture did not really become remarkable until he began to work with a most remarkable client and collaborator, Gertrude Jekyll (1843–1932).

Lutyens first met Miss Jekyll in 1889, the year he began practice. Twenty-six years older than the young architect, she was a disciple of Ruskin who had taken up photography as well as painting and had become increasingly interested in gardening. Living with her mother at Munstead, near Godalming, Gertrude Jekyll took a close interest in the crafts and traditions of Old West Surrey (the title of her book, published in 1904). These were concerns shared by Lutyens, although the 1889 book surveying *Old Cottage and Domestic Architecture in South-West Surrey* by the architect Ralph Nevill suggests a wider interest in the local vernacular. Initially intimidating, intelligent, versatile, erudite and wise, 'Aunt Bumps' as he

called her became hugely important to Lutyens and introduced him, directly or indirectly, to many of his future clients, not least Edward Hudson. As Weaver wrote, 'it would be difficult to exaggerate the importance of her influence'.

Gertrude Jekyll asked Lutyens to design The Hut at Munstead in 1892 as a place to entertain and pursue her own interests, and, in 1895, following the death of her mother and subsequent inheritance of Munstead House (which had been designed by J. J. Stevenson) by her brother Herbert, she commissioned Munstead Wood as a home of her own to be built in the garden she had already established. This was the beginning of a creative collaboration which lasted for almost forty years: 'Miss Jekyll knew very little about architecture and Ned even less about gardening … . Each found in the other the perfect complement.'[21] Lutyens's surviving sketches for the several buildings at Munstead show that Bumps and he had been exploring the possibilities of the Surrey vernacular for several years before Munstead Wood was built. Gertrude Jekyll described the building of her home in her book *House and Garden*, published in 1900, emphasising how

it does not stare with newness; it is not new in any way that is disquieting to the eye; it is neither raw nor callow. On the contrary, it almost gives the impression of a comfortable maturity of something like a couple of hundred years. And yet there is nothing sham-old about it; it is not trumped-up with any specious or fashionable devices of spurious antiquity; there is no pretending to be anything that it is not – no affectation whatever … . The house is not in any way a copy of an old building, though it embodies the general characteristics of the older structures of its own district.[22]

Munstead Wood was published in *Country Life* in 1900 and was very important in Lutyens's career; thanks to Gertrude Jekyll, the

Fisher's Hill, Woking, Surrey (1900 and 1908), designed for Gerald Balfour, the Prime Minister's brother, who had commissioned Lutyens in preference to his own architect brother, Eustace Balfour.

house established his reputation and secured more commissions. For example, William and Julia Chance were about to build nearby, 'but by an unhappy choice,' Mrs Chance later recorded,

we had hit upon an architect [Halsey Ricardo] whose plans we disliked so much that for the moment we had actually given up the idea of building at all, rather than make the irreparable mistake of letting the wrong kind of house materialise. Then a miracle happened. One day on our way to visit our still virgin acres, we walked up the hill from Godalming. Passing through a sandy lane, we saw a house nearing completion, and on the top of a ladder a portly figure giving directions to some workmen. The house was a revelation of unimagined beauty and charm, we stood entranced and gazing, until the figure descended and we found ourselves, after due explanation, being welcomed as future neighbours and shown over the wonderful house – as a result of this meeting we became the owners of a Lutyens house with a Jekyll garden.[23]

This was Orchards. Another result of the encounter was the beginning of the architect's reputation of being rather overanxious to get work.

One admirer of both these romantic creations was Peter Behrens, the future architect of the famous AEG turbine factory in Berlin, who in 1903 wrote to thank Hermann Muthesius for taking him to meet 'Miss Jekyll and Sir Chance' at their Surrey homes and confessed that 'I cannot remember ever having seen so harmonious a union of glorious country, masterly art and human amiability than that at Munstead Wood and Orchards. The English visit was a powerful stimulus to me in many respects. I still feel more and more what a deep impression that "land of culture" made on me; certainly the strongest I have ever had from a country.'[24] Another architect admirer of Munstead Wood was Robert Lorimer (too often patronisingly described as the 'Scottish Lutyens'), who, at the end of 1897, wrote to his friend R. S. Dods in Australia that

Above: The path in front of the south elevation of Gertrude Jekyll's house, Munstead Wood (1895–97).

Left: The south-facing garden front of Orchards at Munstead near Godalming (1897–99), photographed for Country Life *in 1901 soon after its completion.*

... it looks so reasonable, so kindly, so perfectly beautiful, that you feel that people might have been making love, and living and dying there and dear little children running about for the last – I was going to say, thousand years – anyway six hundred. They've used old tiles which of course helps – but the proportion, the way the thing's built – (very low coursed rubble with thick joints, and no corners) – in fact it has been built 'by the old people of the old materials in the old unhurrying way' but at the same time 'sweet to all modern uses' ... and who do you think did this for her – a young chap called Lutyens, twenty-seven he is – and I've always heard him derided by the Schultz school as a 'Society' architect. Miss J. has pretty well run him and now he's doing a roaring trade and has just married a daughter of Lord Lytton, he's evidently right in with the right sort of people – Princess Louise – Lord Battersea etc. etc. and what a Gods mercy that for once in a way these people have got hold of the right man and what a thing for England.[25]

'Schultz' was the Scottish architect Robert Weir Schultz, who had been in the offices of both Norman Shaw and Ernest George, and this letter indicates that, early on, Lutyens's professional and social success provoked jealousy (although, as Schultz's principal client was the Marquess of Bute, he had no real reason to feel aggrieved). However, unlike most of those austere and complex-ridden Arts and Crafts designers, Lutyens had married not only well but comparatively young and had several children. He had met Lady Emily Lytton not, for once, owing to Miss Jekyll but through a family friend, Barbara Webb. They married in August 1897, having eventually overcome the opposition of Emily's mother, the Dowager Countess of Lytton, former Vicereine of India. The honeymoon was spent in Holland, sitting back to back on the beach at Scheveningen. The problems of this marriage have been movingly described by their daughter Mary. To judge by their published correspondence, they got on best when apart, and the physical estrangement between them after the birth of their five children was exacerbated by Lady Emily's involvement in Theosophy and her obsession with Krishnamurti. Before they were engaged, Ned presented Emily with an exquisite casket containing, among other things, the plans of an ideal 'little White House' in the country based on their shared initials: 'E.L.' – an ideal never realised as they always lived in London.

To satisfy the Lytton family, Lutyens had been obliged to take out a life-insurance policy for £11,000, and this contributed to the financial difficulties, incompetently managed, that dogged and worried the architect for the rest of his life. Having leased a large house in Bloomsbury Square after his marriage, Lutyens was keen to take on yet more work. In 1897 he was busy with twenty-five different jobs, including five new houses: Fulbrook, Berry Down, Orchards, Sullingstead and The Pleasaunce at Overstrand. However, although Lutyens had married the daughter of an earl, this did not necessarily advance his career. As Lady Emily wrote after her husband's death, the marriage 'gave him confidence in a social way and gave the world confidence in his abilities', but this intelligent and independent-minded woman refused to play the role of society hostess and ambitious wife.[26] The person who really mattered in this

regard was always the redoubtable and loyal Gertrude Jekyll. As Mary Lutyens pointed out,

Not unnaturally some fellow architects, jealous of Lutyens' extraordinary success, attributed it to the advantages of his marriage ... . In truth he met nearly all his clients directly or indirectly through the Jekylls. Apart from the house he built for his mother-in-law and St Martin's Church, both at Knebworth, the commissions he did get through his wife might equally well have come if he had never met her.[27]

Other commissions, of course, like those for Marsh Court and Papillon Hall, resulted from his exposure in the pages of *Country Life* or from personal recommendation by its proprietor.

'There will never be great architects or great architecture without great patrons,' as Lutyens wrote in his tribute to Philip Webb. This is a truth necessarily evident to architects but too often ignored by architectural historians. Lutyens was fortunate to begin his career when he did, for the decades either side of 1900 were probably the best time ever to find clients for whom to build: there was money around, while labour and materials were comparatively cheap. With his training, his talents and his connections, Lutyens was well placed to respond to the extravagant social needs of that now distant era. As A. S. G. Butler later recalled, 'The period from 1890 to 1914 was probably the richest in the history of the English country-house ... . Living in these houses depended, naturally, on a plentiful supply of servants. The owners' lives were filled partly by voluntary work in the County, a great deal by sport and, to some extent, by the sheer act of living elegantly.'[28]

Lutyens's clients (he preferred to call them 'patrons') were certainly rich – they had to be: he was an expensive architect to employ – but they were not necessarily grand. There were a few peers, but, on the whole, they were not what might at first be expected for an ambitious architect with very good social connections. The 2nd Lord Hillingdon, who built Overstrand Hall, was a banker, while his Norfolk neighbour, Lord Battersea, had been the MP Cyril Flower, whose money came from wool and from his wife, a Rothschild. Gerald Balfour, for whom Lutyens designed Fisher's Hill, was the brother of the Prime Minister and would become the 2nd Earl Balfour, but, after all, the job came because he was married to Lady Emily's older sister. There was Lord Wimborne, of course, but Lutyens's work for him consisted of adding to the magnificent old mansion at Ashby St Ledgers; besides, he was Ivor Guest, of Guest, Keen & Nettlefold, engineers, and the son of an American. An early client was Adeline, Duchess of Bedford, but the job for her was only a garden (designed with Gertrude Jekyll).

At Mells, Lutyens was working for the Horners, who had been there since the reign of Elizabeth I, but at nearby Mells Park, the client was Reginald McKenna, whose family was certainly not old,

Right: *Nashdom, Taplow, Buckinghamshire (1906–08), a whitewashed brick palace for parties on the Thames designed for Princess Alexis Dolgorouki, née Wilson.*

even if he did become a minister in Asquith's government and chairman of the Midland Bank. Only with his late and last big house, Middleton Park (designed in collaboration with his son Robert), did Lutyens build for a member of the old aristocracy in the shape of the Earl of Jersey. It is true that Lutyens could boast one royal client in Princess Louise, Queen Victoria's interesting and artistic daughter, who had been married off to the future Duke of Argyll, but his job for her was to extend an existing building, a small former inn near the big house at Rosneath, down the Clyde. Apart from this Princess, Lutyens's grandest clients were in fact in Spain and Spanish: the Dukes of Alba and Peñaranda. Princess Alexis Dolgorouki, for whom Lutyens designed Nashdom, that great white palace by the Thames, had begun life more prosaically as Fanny Wilson, an heiress from Lancashire. And as for that job at Knebworth for his mother-in-law, the Dowager Lady Lytton, it is not a grand country house at all but an exquisite, brilliant Mannerist cottage: Homewood.

Many of Lutyens's clients, while having aspirations to country gentility (even if only in Surrey), were of the type described by J. Mordaunt Crook in his recent exploration of *The Rise of the Nouveaux Riches* – although few seem to have been foreign or Jewish. Nor were these clients among the richest; as Crook observes, none bequeathed as much as a million pounds before the First World War. This was, in fact, fortunate, as *real* millionaires – 'particularly those with very new money – proved extraordinarily obtuse in the choice of country house architect', that is, they chose duds to build mediocrity.[29] So, although he did not manage to hook any South African diamond tycoons, Lutyens was fortunate in that his patrons were rather more discerning, if typically Edwardian: newish money combined with a sprinkling of those cultivated imperialist bullies who ran the Empire and who, in easy retrospect, can give an unpleasant flavour to the whole period.

Lutyens's first important client, Arthur Chapman of Crooksbury, had returned home from trading in Calcutta to realise his ambition of devoting himself to hunting and being a country gentleman. Gerard Streatfield, cricketer, ornithologist, and the owner of Fulbrook, was perhaps a real gent and did not need to work, but as regards the other famous Surrey houses, William Chance of Orchards was a successful QC with money; Frederick Mirrielees, who built Goddards, became chairman of the Union Castle Line. Tigbourne Court was built for his daughter by (Sir) Edgar Horne, the local MP, chairman of the Prudential Assurance Co. Little Thakeham, in Sussex, which Lutyens once called 'the best of the bunch', was built for Tom Blackburn, who was able to give up being a preparatory-school headmaster when he inherited a fortune and became a country gentleman and gardener.

Perhaps the dodgy clients are more interesting. Archibald Grove, for whom he built that quirky house in Hampshire, Berry Down, was a Liberal MP who had founded the *New Review*; he introduced

Left: *Below the black marble staircase at Heathcote (1906–08), installed by Lutyens in defiance of his client's wishes.*

Lutyens to J. M. Barrie and later commissioned another house, Pollards Wood, but then went bust. And then there was Whitaker Wright, the highly dubious millionaire owner of Witley Park, for whom Lutyens designed a lakeside bathing pavilion and boathouse and who committed suicide after being convicted for fraud. All this and much more can be found in Jane Brown's rich study of *Lutyens and the Edwardians*.

A typical Lutyens client had money from trade or industry, whether made or inherited. Cotton mills were behind Gledstone Hall and wool behind Heathcote; smoking cigarettes paid for Ednaston Manor, and cutting the mustard for haunted Papillon Hall, and wealth from chemicals in Glasgow for Great Maytham; while making lighthouse lenses provided the means for William Chance to build Orchards (and inherit a baronetcy). Mark Fenwick, who rebuilt Abbotswood, was a banker with mining interests; his cousin, Bertie Fenwick, enlarged Temple Dinsley. Other bankers included Cecil Baring as well as Charles Mills, Lord Hillingdon. Herbert Johnson, of Marsh Court, was a stockbroker. Several clients were solicitors, including Cook at Sullingstead, Riddell at The Dormy House (who was also a director of *Country Life* and chairman of the *News of the World*), and Alexander Wedderburn at The Hoo, Willingdon (who, at least, also edited the thirty-eight-volume library edition of the works of John Ruskin with E. T. Cook). Then there were the three bachelor sons (so typical of the period) of the solicitor Sir William Farrer: Gaspard, William and Henry, loyal clients who commissioned both The Salutation at Sandwich and a house in St James's Square.

An exception to the pattern, perhaps, was the well-connected Hon. Alfred Lyttelton, the Old Etonian sportsman son of the 4th Lord Lyttelton of Hagley who, like Gerald Balfour, was one of the 'Souls'. For him Lutyens designed Grey Walls, next to the Muirfield golf course in Scotland. But Lyttelton was not particularly wealthy and he sold this holiday home to Willie James, a crony of King Edward VII who was of American descent and whose wife (in fact, the natural daughter of 'Tum Tum') commissioned Monkton. Other exceptions, perhaps, were the Revd W. H. Evans, the Charterhouse schoolmaster who commissioned The Red House, and the Cambridge don Dr Henry Bond, a friend of Reginald McKenna's, for whom he designed that masterpiece of 'austere beauty', Middlefield. But it is surely significant that the client who, in 1910, asked Lutyens to build him a castle in Devon (near a village associated with imaginary ancestors who had arrived with the Conqueror) was a clergyman's son, Julius Drew, who had been in the tea trade and founded the Home & Colonial Stores but who, dissatisfied with his social position, then added an 'e' to his name.

The world Lutyens felt obliged to move in is suggested by his report to his wife of going to Sonning in 1909 to see a Mr Buckley and finding that 'they are common and vulgar – motors and a launch in the river. Leading a life of absolute idleness punctuated by bridge and racing.'[30] Ideal clients, surely – but the job came to nothing. Perhaps money was not everything. Indeed, what is impressive about

Lutyens and his clients is not only that they would usually return to him when an addition or a new building was required but also that some became friends: not just Hudson, Arthur Chapman and Lady Horner and those to whom he was related by marriage, but Herbert Johnson of Marsh Court, 'Tom' Blackburn, Ivor Guest, Cecil Baring, Mr and Mrs Mark Fenwick, Mrs Merton of Folly Farm and the Farrer brothers as well (although, in 1913, Lady Emily unkindly maintained that 'You are only interested in people while they are building')[31]. He got on well with Mirrielees and wrote to Lady Emily in 1899 that 'Mrs M. is a daughter of Sir D. Currie and will eventually come into a £1,000,000 of money, so they say, so it's, say I, worth business while to "cultivate". This sounds beastly and is, specially as they are really wondrous kind and easy to get on with.' Oswald P. Milne, a former assistant, recalled that 'He had a wonderful way with his clients. He was marvellous not only in dealing with materials but with human beings. He always got them to spend what he wanted them to spend.'[32]

The social and financial character of Lutyens's clientele is not in the least surprising, of course. There was nothing unusual about the new money in Edward VII's tawdry reign; the strength of English society has always been its fluidity and mobility, in which an injection of cash is never unwelcome no matter whence it comes. But perhaps what is most revealing about Lutyens's patrons is the interesting fact that not a single Lutyens house in Great Britain is still lived in by the family that built it: new money moves on, and most are now owned by similar people. The exceptions to this generalisation are, interestingly enough, both abroad (and both built on banking). Lambay Castle, on that remote holiday island near Dublin, is still the property of one of the descendants of Cecil Baring, Lord Revelstoke (whose father had been obliged to give up his Devon seat after the first great Baring crash in 1890), while Lutyens's early and engagingly eccentric essay in France, Le Bois des Moutiers at Varengeville-sur-Mer, is still owned (and opened to the public) by the admirable Mallet family, who were once bankers in Paris and were instrumental in the strange story of Lady Emily Lutyens taking up Theosophy.

There was certainly plenty of money around. Mary Lutyens noted that her father's net income in 1904 was £2,884 and that 'his genius was to find perfect expression in this opulent Edwardian age. It was the age of the great country house, with entertaining from Saturday to Monday. With bathrooms coming into fashion the rich, who did not want to build new houses, at least wanted to alter or enlarge their existing ones (Crooksbury was enlarged twice).' Nikolaus Pevsner put it well when he wrote how Lutyens's 'ideal client was the rich man, preferably self-made or at least not too distant yet in descent from the adventurous stage of self-madeness. And Lutyens was extremely, uniquely fortunate in working at the very last moment in British history when such clients were about.'[33]

The plutocratic Edwardian world that sustained so much new domestic architecture did not, in fact, come to a sudden end in 1914, but conditions certainly changed after the death of Edward VII

in 1910. Lloyd George's 1909 Budget – 'The People's Budget' – increased income tax and death duties and introduced Super-Tax, hitting the sort of people who were Lutyens's best clients. After this date, the architect's career was more concerned with institutional, commercial and official buildings. Lutyens continued to design houses, of course, and two of the grandest – real country houses, in fact: Gledstone Hall and Middleton Park – date from the inter-war years, but after about 1910 the most important clients became the Midland Bank (thanks to Reginald McKenna), the Imperial War Graves Commission, the Roman Catholic Archdiocese of Liverpool and the British government in India.

If not the most representative, perhaps the most sympathetic and poignant of the clients is John Thomas Hemingway, 'who could not spend his money,' Lutyens later remarked, 'until he met me'.[34] He was a self-made Yorkshire businessman, married to a former mill-girl, who had become the owner of George Richardson & Co. of Bradford, and his fortune from exporting wool enabled his fashionable architect to indulge his dream of playing the 'High Game' of Renaissance Classicism – in, of all places, Ilkley. In a celebrated letter to Herbert Baker, Lutyens patronisingly described how he built this palace

in an ultra suburban locality over which villas of dreadful kind and many colours wantonly distribute themselves … . He, the man, wanted cupboards galore, in all rooms, right and left of windows. I wanted something persisting and dominating, with horizontal lines … . To get domination I had to get a scale greater than the height of my rooms allowed, so unconsciously the San Michele invention repeated itself. That time-worn doric order – a lovely thing – I have the cheek to adopt … [35]

And the story goes that Mr and Mrs Hemingway were so pleased with the result that they were happy to hang their clothes over the backs of chairs. But were they? John Brandon-Jones heard that

The client said, 'I don't want a black marble staircase; I want an oak staircase.' Lutyens remarked, 'What a pity.' Later, when they went round the house again, the black marble staircase was installed, and the client protested, 'I told you I didn't want a black marble staircase!' Lutyens replied, 'I know, I said "What a pity" didn't I?' The story is certainly in character, and I hope it is true.[36]

No wonder that Lutyens acquired the unfortunate reputation for being expensive; and no wonder, indeed, that he lost clients to more docile designers – to his dismay, he even lost Princess Louise to his sometime and unsatisfactory business partner (of 1898–1901), E. Baynes Badcock.

The contract price for Heathcote was £17,500. This was a very large sum for a private house, especially when it is considered that the splendid church by Norman Shaw in the same town cost £15,000 less than thirty years earlier. As to convert these prices to a modern equivalent requires adding at least two noughts, such figures can be almost meaningless. What is more indicative of the cost of employing Lutyens is a comparison with the prices of similar contemporary

The garden front of The Hoo, Willingdon, Sussex (1902–03), designed for
Alexander Wedderburn KC, the co-editor of Ruskin's collected writings.

houses by other architects. Unfortunately, for most of Lutyens's jobs the figures are not available, but, on the assumption that his fee was the standard 5 per cent, a note written in 1897 listing anticipated commissions suggests that The Ferry Inn at Rosneath was estimated at £3,000 and Orchards and Fulbrook both at around £5,000. However, the accounts for Fulbrook surviving reveal that the successful tender was for £6,840 and that, in the event, the house (plus stables) cost £9,391, including Lutyens's fee of £459. In comparison, Voysey's nearby Greyfriars cost £4,191 and Lowicks, again in Surrey, even less at £2,137. The Hill House at Helensburgh by Mackintosh came in at £5,975. However, Standen, that big country house by Philip Webb, cost as much as £18,065. In May 1906, Lutyens noted in a letter to his wife that 'Hemingway has signed contract for £17,500, Dolgorouki [Nashdom] accepts £15,000, Birds [Eartham] £7800, Mrs Franklin [New Place] £9300. So this week, signed and sealed, £34,600 … . I am happy at all these jobs coming out right this week as regards prices. But it is only when

they come out right, and the work is to begin, that I wake up to a horror that I have yet to work it all out – and they loom practical and into the realm of the real-to-bes. The worry becomes greater – more, really anxious, but then it is pleasant living the anxiety, and nothing dull.'[37] Rather later, Viceroy's House, New Delhi, cost £877,136 of taxpayers' money at a time when prices were beginning to rise after a long period during which the value of money was stable, although costs were far lower in India. What seems clear is that Mr Hemingway was happy to spend a great deal of money on his new house.

Heathcote is a very grand Italian villa in a district full of Victorian villas; it is not a country house. In fact, Lutyens designed very few proper country houses, or country seats, which is perhaps surprising for an architect so assiduously promoted by *Country Life*. For by the working definition applied by *Country Life* in recent years – that a country house is a residence in the country supported by its estate – very few indeed of Lutyens's houses deserved to be extolled in the pages of the magazine. That they were, of course, was largely owing to his friendship with the editor and proprietor, Edward Hudson. Besides, as John Cornforth points out, the decorative masthead

The Salutation at Sandwich, Kent (1911), a 'Wrennaissance' mansion seen from the centre of town through Lutyens's remarkable gatehouse.

drawn by Byam Shaw and introduced a year after the magazine's foundation in 1897 referred to 'Country Homes – Gardens – Old & New' and that, unlike 'country houses', '"country homes" sounds essentially liveable, and does not necessarily imply a surrounding estate or any historical interest'.[38]

In theory, therefore, *Country Life Illustrated* (as it was called when launched) was interested in new houses as well as old, and in small homes as well as large ones. The first editor knew his audience and their tastes. 'Hudson's flash of genius,' wrote Hussey, '... was to connect the increasing number of people who, like himself, were escaping from towns (some of them in automobiles) to find country life and country homes, with the idea of providing a medium for well-presented advertisements of country residences.'[39] Indeed, *Country Life* was really the pioneering 'lifestyle' magazine, offering its readers a model, a way of life to aspire to and emulate. Old and grand seats, commanding thousands of acres, were illustrated from the beginning to set the desired tone, but they were quite beyond reach. New houses, on the other hand, sited on comparatively small plots in the country but within easy reach of London, were within the bounds of possibility – new traditional houses like Deanery Garden, commissioned by Hudson himself and illustrated almost as an ideal image for his magazine.

Nevertheless, if Lutyens's houses represented the aspirations of many middle-class Englishmen and women who read *Country Life*, they are not the sort of houses that have usually been given coverage in those valuable articles on country seats published over the last century – even if some (Deanery Garden and Marsh Court) somehow crept into Charles Latham's illustrated volumes called *In English Homes*. With very few exceptions, Lutyens's country houses have no estates attached; nor were most of their builders and owners country gentlemen, let alone peers of the realm. No research seems

to have been done into the size of the parcels of land which Lutyens graced with his masterpieces, but it is clear that, no matter how grand the house, most were comparatively small and certainly did not consist of farming land which provided an income for the property (even if such estates had been economically viable at a time of agricultural depression).

In fact, Lutyens – like Frank Lloyd Wright – mostly designed what are best described as *villas*; that is, comparatively small and tightly planned residences which are essentially adjuncts to cities. Almost all of Lutyens's finest houses dating from before the Great War are essentially weekend homes for London commuters; they are exemplars of that very English building type, the middle-class house aspiring to be rural, and so they reflect the snobberies and ambitions of English life. Most were built near railway lines and a high proportion are in Surrey, that notoriously infertile and unaristocratic Home County whose poor soil was being opened up by the railway companies in the third quarter of the nineteenth century to make building plots for metropolitan businessmen. The main line of the London & South Western Railway from Waterloo through Woking was opened in 1838; Guildford was reached in 1845, Farnham and Godalming in 1849 and Haslemere on the 'Direct Portsmouth' line in 1859, while the South Eastern Railway's branch to Reading through Dorking had also opened in 1849. And the houses soon followed. If not strictly suburban, most Lutyens's houses are certainly not truly rural.

Gertrude Jekyll's garden, in which Lutyens built Munstead Wood, close to Godalming and its station, was 15 acres in extent, and most of the building plots in Surrey were considerably smaller. For all its convincing manorial charm, Little Thakeham was built on the edge of only 37 acres of garden, meadow and woodland at a time when serious estates were measured in thousands of acres. Deanery Garden was built for Hudson in an old walled garden near the centre of Sonning, less than 3 acres in extent, which was then treated as a sophisticated formal exemplar. 'House and garden are a single inter-penetrating conception,' as Hussey wrote,

– parts roofed over, others open to the sun, with the garden walks leading right into and about the house, and the windows placed to catch the sparkle of a pool or complete the pattern of a terrace … . Deanery Garden, at once formal and irregular, virtually settled that controversy, of which Sir Reginald Blomfield and William Robinson were for long the protagonists, between formal and naturalistic garden design.

But that does not make it a country house: Capability Brown had operated on a rather larger scale, after all.

Overstrand Hall on the Norfolk coast, like the eccentric and eclectic The Pleasaunce nearby, is essentially a holiday seaside home. Grey Walls, originally High Walls, in Scotland was another, con-veniently sited next to a maritime golf course. Similarly, The Salutation at Sandwich, for all its 'Wrennaissance' formality (to use Lutyens's own term), was a weekend retreat tucked away on a small plot right in the heart of the ancient Kentish port and 'next to a gas works, which was reputed to be good for the asthmatic condition of its owner'.[40] Goddards at Abinger Common was originally built as a holiday 'Home of Rest for Ladies'. Heathcote was squeezed in amongst villas in Ilkley on a 4-acre site created by combining several plots. Monkton in Sussex was certainly rural, but it was a 'trianon', a hot-weather summer retreat on the West Dean estate (with its big house rebuilt by Lutyens's former master, Sir Ernest George). Abbotswood at Stow-on-the-Wold possibly qualified as a country house, but it was an adaptation of a dull, pedestrian Victorian house. Nashdom was built on a mere 13 acres overlooking the Thames and was designed for parties.

Two of Lutyens's grandest houses – Temple Dinsley and Great Maytham – look very imposing indeed, but both were enlargements of Georgian buildings and neither, in fact, lies at the heart of a great estate. Gledstone Hall in Yorkshire and Middleton Park near Bicester certainly were country seats, both replacing Georgian houses, but they were built much later – Middleton just before the Second World War. Before the Great War, only Ednaston Manor, that rather chilly and formal house in Derbyshire, and Castle Drogo, built on 450 acres of glebe lands near Dartmoor, together with (possibly) Marsh Court on its rural site amid fields near Stockbridge in Hampshire, really qualified for inclusion under modern *Country Life* rules.

Lutyens was building at the high tide of the British Empire, from the symbolic needs of which he would benefit so conspicuously in New Delhi. Ironically, perhaps, some of his finest creations – dreams of traditional rural felicity like Deanery Garden – were being conceived and realised during the Boer War, when Britain's brutal and incompetent behaviour towards the Afrikaner republics was provoking the condemnation of the rest of the civilised world. The war in South Africa generated a mood of defensive, paranoid imperialism and exaggerated patriotism, which was certainly

The entrance courtyard at Monkton (1902), Mrs Willie James's 'trianon' near West Dean in Sussex.

reflected in architecture. The principal manifestation was urban, in the attempt to make London vie with Paris and Berlin as a capital city, but domestic architecture was also affected. Lutyens was far from the only architect to move from a creative adaptation of free 'Tudor' to the reassuring formal certainties of the legacy of Sir Christopher Wren and the Georgian in these years.

Writing in 1913, when an intolerant, arrogant nationalism – in Britain just as in Germany – was making a war in Europe increasingly likely, Weaver was concerned to emphasise the Englishness of Lutyens's art while also recognising its individuality. 'Vital art dare not keep to narrow paths or the traditions of the elders in any one selected style,' he wrote in his introduction to *Houses and Gardens by E. L. Lutyens.*

The Ferry Inn at Rosneath (1896–97), for H.R.H. Princess Louise, as illustrated by Hermann Muthesius in his three-volume study of Das englische Haus *(1904).*

Such houses as New Place, Shedfield, are conceived in the spirit of broad and dateless English traditions, yet with subtle differences in treatment which stamp it as the work of a modern. Others, like Great Maytham and The Salutation, Sandwich, are alive with all the wide humanism of the age of Wren … . Yet through it all there runs the vein of a marked personality, ever busy in invention and full of humour.

Yet invention must not be taken too far and, after the Great War, the insular conservatism of English domestic architecture became even more entrenched. Architects looked back to the golden Edwardian period, when standards of building craftsmanship were high and costs low. In the 1920s, when Lutyens designed Gledstone Hall, the ideal remained sober and restrained, whether in a gentlemanly Palladian or a rustic, vernacular Arts and Crafts manner. Innovation and foreign influences were not welcomed: the war had been fought, after all, to keep England free of German domination. In 1921, in the second volume of his *Small Country Houses of Today* (published by *Country Life*), Sir Lawrence Weaver could actually

The Pleasaunce at Overstrand (1897–98), a rambling eccentricity for Lord Battersea within which two Victorian villas somewhere lie buried.

insist that 'A new method of design is incredible, simply because it is not feasible. We had our misfortunes a few years ago in that pursuit, but even before the war the "New Art" which pleased Germany and Austria so vastly was "dead and damned" in Great Britain.' So it was, but such blinkered jingoism was to falsify history, for the fact remained that Weaver's hero, Edwin Lutyens, had once himself been interested in the 'New Art', even if *Country Life* didn't really want to know.

Like A. S. G. Butler, who, in the 1950 *Lutyens Memorial* interpreted Lutyens's work according to his own prejudices and taste for Classicism, Weaver and Hudson had their own *Country Life* view of Lutyens's achievement. They clearly wanted to see his work as supremely English, for what is conspicuous is that his more eccentric and less reticent *fin de siècle* creations – those houses which make him directly comparable with, say, Charles Rennie Mackintosh – were censored. Writing about Marsh Court in 1906, L. March Phillips was pleased to find 'a complete absence of, what one meets with so frequently in modern work, an over-anxious and ingenious originality'. Weaver evidently did not like those elongated oriels or those

curious glazed corner turrets that appear at both The Ferry Inn at Rosneath and in Varengeville-sur-Mer, and, indeed, the very few surviving photographs of other houses exhibiting such eccentric features in the *Country Life* collection seem never to have been published. Weaver ignored The Ferry Inn and The Red House, that small, strange and extraordinary hillside castle at Godalming, while including but one small photograph of Le Bois des Moutiers (Butler ignored all three). Yet Hermann Muthesius illustrated The Ferry Inn in *Das englische Haus* and for H. S. Goodhart-Rendel, it was here at Rosneath that 'we first feel there is magic in the air'.[41]

A more balanced survey of Lutyens's late-Victorian and Edwardian houses turns up many features which, if not actually Art Nouveau, are certainly like some more extreme Arts and Crafts buildings in their invention and eccentricity. But such things were not English or gentlemanly enough for Weaver, or perhaps even for Miss Jekyll. It was as if Lutyens could only let his hair down when well away and out of sight from Surrey. However, that inventive but oddly disjointed early house, Berry Down, which was again ignored by Weaver, was not so far away in Hampshire, and its architect seems to have allowed it to be published in W. Shaw Sparrow's book on *The Modern Home* as well as in *The Studio*. Even so, perhaps it was Lutyens himself who wished to suppress the memory of some of his early experiments? He would not have been the first, and certainly not the last famous architect who tried to rewrite his own history.

In his 1913 book, Weaver noted that those long oriels at Le Bois des Moutiers were 'an echo of Norman Shaw'. They are, for they were a development of the windows on the façade of the famous Swan House on the Chelsea Embankment. But they are more than that. What Lutyens's work at both Varengeville and Rosneath reveals is an interest in the more experimental architecture of the 1890s, such as the houses of C. F. A. Voysey, which represented, as he later recalled, 'an old world made new and with it, to younger men, of whom I was one, the promise of a more exhilarating sphere of invention'.[42] And then, perhaps, there were also the remarkable designs in Scotland by the principal British exponent of the Art Nouveau. On his way to Rosneath in 1897, Lutyens passed through Glasgow and visited Miss Cranston's new Buchanan Street tea-rooms designed by George Walton and decorated by Mackintosh, finding it 'all very elaborately simple on very new school High Art Lines', as he reported to his fiancée. 'The result gorgeous! And a wee bit vulgar! She has nothing but green handled knives and all is curiously painted and coloured.'

A year later he was back, enjoying 'cheap clean foods in surroundings prompted by the New Art Glasgow School. Green, golds, blues, white rooms with black furniture, black rooms with white furniture, where Whistler is worshipped and Degas tolerated, Rodin extolled for his sic impertinence and admired for the love of oddity, sometimes called originality.'[43] Hussey quoted this letter to demonstrate Lutyens's 'instinctive yet imaginative conservatism, which ... modern art was apt to repel'. Yet Lutyens went on to write that 'It's all clever and original ... . The food! etc. at a third of the cost and three times better than the ordinary hotel, and the surroundings full of space for fancy and amusement. There is tradition of every country and I believe planet! Of the universe – yet

The symmetrical north elevation of The Pleasaunce with its curious Art Nouveau oriel windows.

tis all one.' There is no doubt that Lutyens was affected by his experience of the Glasgow 'New Art' and, after all, he himself would go in for black walls and unusual, dramatic colour combinations – in Bloomsbury Square, at Folly Farm, and elsewhere. As Hussey, if not Weaver, recognised, 'with its tall slender oriel lights, some of them used hinge-like at the angles, the Varengeville house is another instance of that hesitation in his development which, if pursued, might have transformed the course of English architecture in the Edwardian decade'.

In the event, however, he was to pursue a very different course. At a time when, all over Europe, architects like Victor Horta and Josef Hoffmann were abandoning the Art Nouveau or the *Jugendstil* in favour of something more formal and disciplined, Lutyens took up the Grand Manner or the 'High Game'. He was not the first to do this, but others followed him. John Brandon-Jones recalled that 'Voysey regarded Lutyens as by far the most promising architect of the younger generation. Years later he said that it was a disaster that Lutyens turned to the Renaissance and that other young men followed his lead. He believed that if Lutyens had not defected to the Classical Camp, England might have developed a sound modern architecture of her own.'[44] And Hussey seemed to agree when, looking back to the turn of the century from the vantage point of 1932, he observed that Lutyens,

after a decade of flirting with picturesque cottages clad in russet tile and bonneted with gables, was walking out with that demure Georgian lady descended from Queen Anne, whom he was to crown long afterwards with an imperial dome at Delhi ... . Her descendants have become as the sand on the seashore. Although, before they set up house together, she had already consorted with Norman Shaw and Philip Webb in their old age, and even given counsel to William Morris, yet it is principally owing to Sir Edwin Lutyens' long championship of the new Queen Anne that English architecture took the direction that it did during the first generation of the twentieth century ... . And, whatever the direction taken by architecture in the future, it is the personality and influence of Sir Edwin Lutyens that will be recognised as the dominating force in England during the first quarter of the century.[45]

As we have seen, Lutyens had begun with the Surrey-Tudor-vernacular – with what Hussey recognised could descend into 'quaintness' – and his early houses, with their patches of half-timber, show the influence of his sometime master, Ernest George. More important to the creative development of his work were the examples set by Webb and Shaw. He was also, inevitably, strongly influenced by the architectural writings of the great Ruskin, which even affected his attitude to Classical architecture. Lutyens's first mature house, Munstead Wood, demonstrated how he – and his equally important client – shared the ideals of the Arts and Crafts movement, for it is superbly built with local stone and other local materials. As Gertrude Jekyll herself described,

Some heavy oak timber-work forms a structural part of the inner main framing of the house. Posts, beams, braces, as well as doors and their frames, window-frames and mullions, stairs and some floors, are of good English oak, grown in the neighbourhood. I suppose a London builder could not produce such work. He does not go into the woods and buy the standing timber, and season it slowly in a roomy yard for so many years, and then go round with the architect's drawing and choose the piece that exactly fits the purpose ... . Though the work of the London builder is more technically perfect, it has none of the vigorous vitality and individual interest of that of the old countryman, and all ways of working according to local tradition are necessarily lost.[46]

Brick, tile and timber: the centre of the west front of New Place, Shedfield, Hampshire (1905–06).

No wonder that the name of the builder – Thomas Underwood – was cut into the stone wall below the half-timbered projecting gallery at Munstead Wood. Then followed, in rapid succession, Lutyens's supreme early masterpieces, including Orchards and Deanery Garden: houses which, while controlled by the pursuit of more abstract and formal ideas, exhibit the superb building craftsmanship which puts their architect firmly in the Arts and Crafts fold. Orchards is arguably the most brilliant and sophisticated house of the 1890s, in which the complex, formal gardens are linked to the house by sight-lines and axes. Here, the resonances of the vernacular, rustic style and the exquisite use of building materials enhance a remarkably abstract and inventive formal conception. While illustrating Orchards in *Das englische Haus*, Muthesius commented that

The surprising thing about his exteriors is their unusually simple and spacious style and excellent treatment of the materials, in which he is the undisputed master. He manages to give unexpected charm to a simple stone wall, a brick or half-timbered wall ... . These houses are as convincing in their workmanlike efficiency as in their intimate, pleasing appearance and are undoubtedly among the best built in England today.

Part of the greatness of Lutyens is that he was not just a paper architect. Charming and powerful as his sketches are, it is the three-

dimensional reality of his buildings that matters, and that reality depends upon the careful, harmonious and witty use of the best building materials – stone, brick, tile, timber, plaster and lead. 'The colour of buildings has both a chromatic and a sculptural sense,' Lutyens observed. 'You cannot go far wrong in building-colour if you use local materials ... . There is wit, and may be humour, in the use of material.' He later sympathised with the desire for 'something fresh, something better' evident in work of young architects committed to the Modern Movement, but he found the results 'to lack style and cohesion, besides being unfriendly and crude'. As for new materials,

I enjoy all construction, and the steel girder with its petticoat of concrete is a most useful ally in the ever recurring advent of difficulty. The thin walls are worth while, if only to watch your Client's face glow with joy at winning a few square feet of carpet. But I crave for soft thick noiseless walls of hand-made brick and lime, the deep light reflecting reveals, the double floors, easy stairways, and doorways never less than 1 ft. 6 ins. from a corner. The waste of space, which unwittingly creates that most valuable asset, a gain of space.'[47]

No wonder that for the young Henry-Russell Hitchcock, writing a quarter of a century later than Muthesius, 'In the Deanery Garden ... Lutyens may almost be said to have built all unwittingly the finest house of the New Tradition. It is surely one of the finest pieces of traditional craftsmanship produced in the twentieth century.'[48]

Brick, tile, timber and creeper: the porch at Fisher's Hill, the house designed for Lady Emily Lutyens's sister and brother-in-law.

A Georgian house made overwhelmingly neo-Georgian: Temple Dinsley, Hertfordshire (1908–09), enlarged for Mrs Bertie Fenwick.

After the turn of the century, however, and after experimenting with the possibilities of the 'New Art', Lutyens may have got bored with reinterpreting the Surrey vernacular – the language of cottages and barns – and, finding the picturesque too easy, was seeking to engage with a more challenging and geometrical language of form. He soon responded to the growing taste for the monumental and the Classical, which we call 'Edwardian Baroque'. And the houses certainly got bigger. As early as 1903 he was writing that 'In architecture Palladio is the game!! It is so big – few appreciate it now, and it requires training to value and realise it. The way Wren handled it was marvellous. Shaw has the gift. To the average man it is dry bones, but under the hand of a Wren it glows and the stiff materials become as plastic clay.'[49]

Lutyens had introduced a Palladian (or French Neo-Classical?) touch in the form of rusticated Doric columns at Papillon Hall, but the turning point would seem to be Heathcote, Mr Hemingway's unlikely *palazzo* in Ilkley. This was the house, designed in 1905, in which, inspired by Sanmicheli, he famously experimented with 'that

time-worn doric order …'. 'You can't copy it. To be right you have to take it and design it … . It means hard labour, hard thinking, over every line in all three dimensions and in every joint; and no stone can be allowed to slide. If you tackle it in this way, the order belongs to you, and every stroke, being mentally handled, must become endowed with such poetry and artistry as God has given you.'[50] This letter alone explains why Lutyens's Classical houses have an intellectual coherence and dynamism entirely lacking from the pedestrian work of the several more recent fashionable country-house architects who fondly imagine they are following in the footsteps of Palladio.

'Only a villa, but how grand the treatment!' observed Nikolaus Pevsner, who was always ambivalent towards Lutyens's work. 'The house marks the change in Lutyens's style from the Voysey-Tudor-Arts-and-Crafts to the Classical-Palladian-Georgian, but the treatment is as free as any of Lutyens, and the mannerisms of the later work are still absent.'[51] But for Hitchcock, that other censorious modernist, Heathcote was the moment when 'Lutyens surrendered completely to revivalism'.[52] The story, in fact, is not so simple. Not only did Lutyens never try another complex Mannerist palace like Heathcote, preferring to use a much simpler 'Wrennaissance' manner in his later Edwardian houses like The Salutation, Great

White render, special thin bricks and a curious duality either side of the dominating chimney-stack: Barton St Mary, Forest Row, Sussex (1906), for G. Munro Miller.

Maytham and Ednaston Manor, but he had been using Classical elements, and playing games with them, much earlier – almost from the beginning, in fact. For, in truth, the revival of Classicism in Edwardian Britain dates not from the military and moral disgrace of the Boer War but from at least a decade earlier. Bryanston, Norman Shaw's Baroque pile for the Duke of Portman, had been built back in 1889–94.

Furthermore, there is no easy chronological sequence in Lutyens's use of different styles. Writing in 1950, Butler gave comparatively little space to the early work in the *Country Houses* volume of the *Lutyens Memorial* and discussed what was, for him, the welcome move towards Classicism in his second chapter entitled 'Increasing Symmetry in Design' – as if that was all that really mattered in his architecture. In fact, of course, even behind his symmetrical façades, Lutyens's plans are cleverly and deliberately asymmetrical. It surely says more about Butler than it does about his hero that it was the one

big new symmetrical (pompous) house in which the central axis was uninterrupted from front to back, Gledstone Hall, that he considered 'a work of art worthy to be listed, one day, as a national monument'. Lutyens, Butler insisted, 'strove more and more to imbue his work with that note of total harmony in design without which there can be no perfection'. But this interpretation, of course, was to dismiss that crucial aspect of Lutyens: his ability to compose asymmetrically with masterly balance which was rooted in the English Picturesque tradition; it was also crudely to simplify a complex story.

Folly Farm in Berkshire seems to be a superb example of Lutyens's vernacular manner, with sweeping planes of tiled roof coming down almost to the ground to enclose a cloister around two sides of a pool, to which a demure little symmetrical William and Mary wing has later been added. But, in actual fact, the Classical house came *first* – built in 1906 for H. H. Cochrane – and what Lutyens called his 'cowsheds' were added as late as 1912 for a new owner, Zachary Merton, an elderly industrialist (whose German Theosophist wife knew Lady Emily), to provide a dining room and some more bedrooms and bathrooms. 'For sheer originality the Folly Farm twins are unique even in Lutyens repertory,' thought Hussey.

'The clash could have been deplorable.' Of course it would have been difficult to add to a perfect, symmetrical house, so Lutyens built in a contrasting style to make the new conspicuously different from the old (and so conforming, no doubt inadvertently, to the principles of Morris's Society for the Protection of Ancient Buildings). Similarly reversing the conventional historical process, when Lutyens altered Crooksbury for a new owner in 1914, he converted the neo-Georgian wing of 1898 into streamlined-roughcast-Tudor.

With that grasp of essentials, that intuitive understanding of the possibilities of formal, grammatical architectural language, Lutyens was a natural Mannerist – in the Italian Renaissance sense, able to subvert expectations – almost from the beginning. Lutyens's own way of putting this was to state that 'Architecture is building with wit' and that 'There is that in art which transcends all rules, it is the divine … . [W]ith inspiration rules are forgotten and some immeasurable cycle of law is followed, unconsciously by some unaccounted impulse – in my own work and with the moderns.'[53] Lutyens played games – both with different styles and within the logic and meaning of each style: another of his aphorisms was 'One of the elements of beauty is Surprise'. It is the wit in Lutyens's buildings which delights, although it can also exasperate: it was a reflection of his character, his eternal youthfulness and playfulness, of which staid old Herbert Baker eventually tired. Perhaps the best example of a joke that can go stale are those pilasters which 'disappear' into continuous rustication which first appeared at Heathcote and which later so irritated Pevsner when he first encountered such 'silly tricks'. As Goodhart-Rendel wrote of Lutyens, 'By his extraordinary accomplishment he brought the Classical orders completely under his control, a rare achievement in an Englishman, but his perpetual boyishness led him sometimes to play Classical pranks the humour of which may pall.'[54]

Lutyens's formal inventiveness bubbled up from the beginning and never flagged. At Orchards, he indulged in false, open, functionless dormer windows as motifs; at Overstrand Hall, at about the same time, he demonstrated his ability to abstract and deconstruct

Maintaining the integrity of roof and wall planes: Millmead, Bramley, Surrey (1905–06), built as a speculation for Gertrude Jekyll.

the elements of the Classical language in the entrance arch in which the inner arch hangs free in space, held in position by a few voussoir stones. It was an idea he developed in the entrance to Marsh Court and with that jointed flat arch with a keystone which runs across the chord of the segmental pediment above the front door of Homewood. He was still playing with this theme of deconstructed Classicism in some of his very last works – like the Australian Memorial at Villers-Bretonneaux near Amiens. Even Lutyens's early vernacular houses could be handled with a Mannerist sense of form in the novel disposition of Classicised geometrical elements – as on the remarkable end elevation of Le Bois des Moutiers or on the additions he made to Abbotswood. Furthermore, Classical columns and rustication often appear inside houses which, externally, seem pure vernacular Tudor, like Fulbrook, Little Thakeham or even

The back of Ednaston Manor, Derbyshire (1912–14), appearing as if Georgian enlargements were wrapped around a much older house.

Marsh Court, while on the entrance front of Tigbourne Court – that masterpiece of pure geometrical form carried out in rugged local stone and brick – a Hardwick Hall-style Doric order appears below the central three gables. It is often this fusion of different styles, in compositions of breathtaking formal control, which can make Lutyens's houses so thrilling and fresh, while remaining quintessentially English.

Combining Classical columns with rustic walling is an aspect of Lutyens's work which has been described as 'paradox'. What might seem conventional in his houses is often undermined or contradicted by something unexpected, such as the deliberate blocking of a main axis or, at Nashdom, by deflating the symmetrical formality of the principal elevation by lowering the parapet in the middle and by having a void in the centre of the plan. The playing of games, the mannerism in Lutyens's compositions, was all part of subverting rules and expectations, which is why he should never be dismissed as a conventional, predictable knighted architect – like Sir Reginald

Blomfield or Sir Herbert Baker, perhaps. As Peter Inskip has written, 'While several of Lutyens's houses suffer from pomposity and predictability because of their programme and the use of a basic planning approach, the best houses avoid this through the use of paradox: much of the enjoyment of these houses largely depends on the contradiction of an idea established within the design.'[55]

On the other hand, this combining of different styles can seem contrived, even tiresome, in that it may represent an attempt to build in fake history. There was nothing new in this: houses by George Devey of half a century earlier sometimes incorporated patches of rubble stone in walls of brick, as if a new house had been raised on the ruins of a dissolved monastery in Tudor times. Built-in history, suggesting a long pedigree, has a long history in English domestic architecture and naturally appealed to the sort of new money for whom Devey, like Lutyens, worked. This quality in Lutyens's houses, which Inskip defines as 'Archaeology', manifests itself not only in the use of a Tudor style, traditionally crafted in timber and brick, but in the deliberate combination of styles. At Homewood, an Ionic villa has seemingly been overwhelmed by vernacular additions, while at the back of Ednaston Manor the gables of an older house are apparently enclosed by Georgian improvements.

Lutyens once observed that 'the visible result of time is a large factor in realised aesthetic value', but, although he liked using building materials that soon weathered well, he did not indulge in that wholesale faking of olde-worlde charm characteristic of neo-Tudor houses of the 1920s. Lutyens played with images, with the idea of history, handling historical references with sophistication and wit, and thereby raising his traditional-looking buildings from the merely contrived and pretentious to the level of serious architecture. Even so, it should not be forgotten that Lutyens was prepared to indulge in what Weaver called 'reconstituting ancient architecture' when asked. For the 'English' Pavilion at the Paris Exposition of 1900, he designed a reconstruction of Kingston House, an Elizabethan mansion at Bradford-on-Avon – which must have made a telling, if ludicrous, contrast with the Art Nouveau and National Romantic pavilions erected by more adventurous countries – while at

Above: *Aggrandisement of a dull Victorian pile: the new entrance wing added to Abbotswood, Stow-on-the-Wold, Gloucestershire (1901–02), for Mark Fenwick.*

Right: *The churchyard at Ashby St Ledgers, Northamptonshire, with the tomb of Lord Wimborne (d. 1939) and one of the memorial crosses Lutyens had designed for the Imperial War Graves Commission.*

Lutyens at Ashby St Ledgers:

Top: *The old Manor House with its new right-hand wing (1904).*

Middle: *The new dining-room wing mixing happily with older buildings (1924).*

Below: *A group of six thatched cottages in the village (1908).*

Earl's Court in 1912, Lutyens created what were essentially real stage sets for the 'Shakespeare's England' exhibition.

Several of Lutyens's important works were, in fact, enlargements and alterations of old buildings. The core of Ruckmans is an old farm-house, while the powerful, Mannerist work at Abbotswood was an addition to a dull Victorian house. At Lindisfarne, he adapted an existing castle. Lutyens's most archaeological exercise was Great Dixter in Sussex where, for Nathaniel Lloyd, the future author of *A History of English Brickwork* and historian of the English House as well as an important *Country Life* contributor, he restored a fifteenth-century timber-framed house and added to it another timber house rescued from Benenden in Kent. In a very different vein, both Temple Dinsley and Great Maytham were enlargements of existing Georgian houses.

Perhaps Lutyens's happiest combination of new and old is to be found at Ashby St Ledgers in Northamptonshire, where the estate had been bought by the Hon. Ivor Guest, later the 1st Viscount Wimborne. The Elizabethan house was altered and enlarged to give it a symmetrical garden front, while new buildings were added including an old timber-framed house rescued from Ipswich and a new dining-room wing in a streamlined-Tudor style. Lutyens also worked elsewhere in the village, designing a house for Guest's land agent and a charming row of six thatched cottages – Lutyens was a master of small houses as well as large. Finally, in the wooded churchyard, he designed Lord Wimborne's tomb next to a version of the thin, flat standing crosses he had designed for the Imperial War Graves Commission, both combining to make a powerful, poignant statement in pure, abstract, resonant geometry carried out in Portland stone, which seems so right in its elegiac setting.

Lutyens's ability to pursue inventive, expressive games with the Classical language, despite – or perhaps because of – his lack of academic training, surely make him a true Mannerist, like the Italian Renaissance architects whose work (until 1909) he only knew from photographs; he was certainly the cleverest manipulator of Classical forms in Britain since Vanbrugh and Hawksmoor. His own interpretations of 'Edwardian Baroque' are very different from the dry, pedantic essays by those contemporary architects who wished to reform architecture on academic, Beaux-Arts lines. His sheer inventiveness is perhaps most evident in his chimneypieces. Surely no other architect created so many and such witty variations on the theme of the open fireplace and hood. Back in the 1890s, in early houses like Munstead Wood, he experimented with geometrical forms such as convex coves and arches, executed in brick, and in all his houses he explored the possibilities of arches and rustication, of patterned brickwork and keystones, of stepped-back canopies and timber lintels, of panels and niches, of recessions and concavities, even of towers and battlements. The style would often be appropriate to the house, so at Castle Drogo the carefully jointed stone lintels make a chimneypiece look like a medieval gatehouse, while in Viceroy's House, variety was achieved by Mannerist and Baroque variations on more conventional Classical forms of chimneypiece.

Top: *House and garden inseparable: the new west front at Abbotswood.*

Above: *Restoration and re-erection: Great Dixter (1910), built for Nathaniel Lloyd.*

But there are always surprises: a fireplace inside Overstrand Hall, constructed of brick, stone and timber, is as brilliant and weird as anything by Michelangelo. A Lutyens chimneypiece is architecture as abstract sculpture.

And then there are the chimneys – tall, massive, magisterial pylons or obelisks, ostensibly functional but in fact disposed carefully and precisely so as to hold a composition together (often regardless of interior convenience). Middlefield is dominated by and yet not overawed by three colossal chimneys, placed symmetrically and precisely in line: it would be a poorer building without them. This is a house designed just a couple of years after Heathcote, yet there are no pilasters and there is no Classical order. The architecture is simplified Georgian fused with the sweeping roofs of vernacular cottages and barns; the style is, in fact, just pure Lutyens carried out in special thin bricks. Middlefield reveals him as a master of abstract, pure form in brick and tile. Chimneys rise to the sky while vast, unbroken planes of tiled roof accommodate themselves to projection and recession, rise and fall, to descend almost to the ground. The result is an awesomely precise and balanced architectural

Dignity and abstraction in brick for a Cambridge don: Middlefield, Stapleford, Cambridge (1908–09), designed for Dr Henry Bond.

composition and yet is unmistakeably domestic in character: inviting, comfortable, secure. And the architect was justifiably proud: 'I have, for a little house, got an extraordinary amount of dignity into it'.[56] The pity is, perhaps, that Lutyens did not develop this manner to create what could have been a distinctively modern domestic architecture balanced between tradition and abstraction.

In comparison with the eclectic freedom of his Tudor houses, however, and even with the Mannerist fireworks at Heathcote, some of the later, larger Edwardian houses may seem a little dry and lifeless – but they were not Lutyens's only preoccupation at that time. For while he was interested in formal geometry in homage to his heroes – Sanmicheli, Palladio and Wren – the romantic side of his nature achieved fulfilment by building castles: the most exciting castles raised since the days of Fonthill and Peckforton, and rather more comfortable internally. There were the restoration and

enlargement of Lindisfarne Castle perched on its rock on Holy Island for his ideal client, Edward Hudson, and there was a similar job at an even more ruined castle on Lambay Island for Cecil Baring. Both, perhaps, owe something to Stokesay Castle, which Lutyens and Herbert Baker had sketched back in 1890 and which he never forgot. The excitingly abstract compositions of geometrical, military forms that enliven the roofscapes of his castles can certainly be traced back to that most romantic pile in Shropshire.

Lutyens had first used a streamlined-Tudor style as early as 1897–98 for that unsung masterpiece by Charterhouse School, the brick Red House at Godalming, but the severe military style Lutyens evolved also owed something to Charles Holden's Bristol Central Library, published in 1906. It was also used at Penheale Manor in Cornwall and for that most austere mansion, Abbey House at Barrow-in-Furness, built for Messrs Vickers, the armaments manufacturer, to put up visitors to their works. This was the first house to be written up for *Country Life* by Christopher Hussey (in 1921) and, as Cornforth observes, the article is interesting because it shows how he had picked up an essential thread in Tipping's and Weaver's work before the War – the search for a style for today. At the end he wrote, 'the brilliance of the design lies in the fact that the house satisfies both schools of thought in that it is essentially Jacobean and undeniably Lutyens. And in this elasticity of style lies, I think, the great hope of modern architecture'.[57]

But the supreme manifestation of Lutyens's castle style is, of course, Castle Drogo, that astonishing essay in the sculptural handling of planes of granite – inside as well as out – in which the corridors seem more exciting than the principal rooms. The planning of Drogo is odd because, vast as it is, what stands today is an incomplete fragment, largely owing to the death of the client's son and heir in the Great War. Even so, it is the supreme manifestation of what Pevsner – able to see England with detachment – concluded was the explanation for the great success of an apparently whimsical eccentric like Lutyens:

the fascination wrought on the British more than any other race by the folly in architecture. Nor need the British be ashamed of that fascination; for to appreciate folly and a folly a degree of detachment is needed which is only accessible to old and humane civilizations. Sir Edwin Lutyens was without doubt the greatest folly builder England has ever seen. Castle Drogo beats Fonthill ...[58]

Yet, surprisingly perhaps, this was not something Lutyens wanted to design in 1910: 'Only I do wish he didn't want a Castle,' he wrote of Mr Drew(e), 'but just a delicious loveable house with plenty of good large rooms in it.'[59]

Lutyens was a master at arranging and combining good large rooms. His houses were superbly planned for the purpose for which they were designed, which was, essentially, to entertain at weekends. This involved 'respecting the privacy and comfort of guests through a hieratic arrangement dividing the house between guests, family and staff', to quote Peter Inskip, who has made a careful study of his plan forms. He concludes that Lutyens's houses

all possess the basic plan elaborated to accommodate the specific programme and overlaid with stylistic quotations from historical and contemporary sources, producing an 'original' design. The basic plan is common to the majority of his projects for houses ... and the pattern established in those built early in his career around Godalming in Surrey is modified only in response to the differing requirements of more affluent clients and the development of the group of architectural ideas he was exploring.

The typical house required three distinct groups of rooms: a suite of reception rooms, including perhaps a double-height Great Hall; a private retreat for the owners to escape from their guests, usually a library; and the kitchens and other functional spaces. All three needed to be separate and yet connected. Unlike a Georgian or Victorian country-house architect, Lutyens would usually arrange the reception rooms to face south, to catch the sun. And these rooms would not be simple rectangles but spaces made more complex,

Almost the last: Halnaker House near Chichester, Sussex (1936–38), for an old and loyal client, Reginald McKenna.

Abstract sculpture: the severely military roofscape of Castle Drogo, perhaps a reminiscence of Stokesay Castle in Shropshire.

perhaps by the addition of generous window bays or even by being L-shaped in plan. The entrance, ideally, would be at the north, but if this was impossible there would be a shift in axis.

What is conspicuous is that Lutyens's plans were never simply symmetrical or axial. To arrive at and enter one of his houses was to undertake a journey, passing over a deliberate threshold (which might be a formal, external space) and then to make a circuitous route to the principal reception room. Sometimes the movement was vertical, as in the brilliant Red House at Godalming, built on the side of a steep hill, in which the rooms are arranged in a rectangular spiral around a central, gentle open staircase. As Inskip observes, there is a hierarchical arrangement of spaces 'within the protected area very similar to that of a medieval castle organised about its keep'. And sometimes the climax of the journey – which might involve up to eight turns – would not be the Great Hall but the garden terrace.

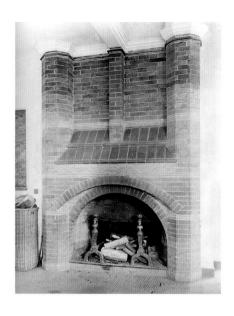

A MISCELLANY OF
CHIMNEYPIECES

(opposite page):

Top: *Daneshill,
Munstead Wood,
Ruckmans.*

Middle: *Lindisfarne Castle,
Castle Drogo (twice).*

Bottom: *Middleton Park,
Little Thakeham.*

(this page):

Top: *Folly Farm,
Viceroy's House,
Ednaston Manor.*

Middle: *Heathcote.*

Bottom: *Castle Drogo,
Gledstone Hall,
Viceroy's House.*

The smart and symmetrical entrance lodges at Middleton Park (1934–38), the country seat Lutyens rebuilt for the Earl of Jersey.

Lutyens was not interested in the open plan that Frank Lloyd Wright adopted in houses that were purely for family use. But, like Wright, he often placed a solid core, containing a fireplace, in the centre of his house plan – as at Heathcote – around which the visitor navigated through doors between rooms. And, again like Wright, Lutyens was a master at extending his house into the landscape, linking house and garden both through solid elements, like projecting walls, and through dominant visual axes extended outside through doors or windows. This was something that Muthesius observed, noting how 'in siting a house he seeks to relate as closely as possible to the surrounding terrain by developing the architectonic idea in the form of terraces and flower-beds, pools, box-hedges and pergolas'. But while Wright's prairie houses extend into space yet seemingly float free above open, flat land, Lutyens integrated his architecture into the landscape and created a series of enclosed spaces around the house. Sometimes these spaces are at different levels, separated by retaining walls, so that, in the *Country Life* photographs, it is sometimes difficult to relate one view to another.

Part of Lutyens's genius was – with the help of Gertrude Jekyll – to treat gardens as architecture, exploiting different levels, linked by

clever steps which are exemplars of formal geometry, or extending the building into space through pergolas, walls or even detached piers. Barriers were placed to shield both house and garden from the outside world, sometimes making a 'fortified site' containing a series of walls and courts (*The Secret Garden* by Frances Hodgson Burnett was inspired by Great Maytham, where the old walled garden was incorporated by Lutyens into his design). This is apparent in his several houses in his abstracted-castle style, but also in his more formal and sober designs inspired by the Classicism of Wren. Such plans are an invitation to explore and to enter: Grey Walls, with its concave façade reconciling diagonal and rectilinear geometries, is the supreme example of this. And the required movement into and through the house increases its apparent size – the concern which is also so evident in the carefully composed *Country Life* photographs.

In a study of Lutyens's houses, John Rollo has identified three basic plan types: the 'Stepped', the 'Simple Linear' and the 'Elizabethan Hybrid' plans. His later plans are wonderfully compact within their envelopes, and clearly reflect the study of Italian

Renaissance masters, although, having to respond to much more complex requirements, he never adopted Palladio's simple symmetries. Nevertheless, Lutyens increasingly relied on proportional systems in his work which he partly derived from Renaissance manuals (while, for detail, the 'office bible' was the *City and Country Builder's and Workman's Treasury of Designs* of 1740 by Batty Langley). Invited to buy books for the Public Works Department in India in 1921, Lutyens wanted to acquire 'only those that Wren could have had access to but of what use is it to buy any book he did not know until we are able to do better than what he did. The tons of art publication might just as well go to the sea – save for the record.'[60]

Even at the beginning of his career, Lutyens seems to have used basic proportional systems in his house plans and it is surely significant that he worked out his designs on squared paper. Rollo has established that three-quarters of all his principal rooms conform to Palladio's six rectilinear plan proportions. The use of pure geometry, with intimidatingly precise measurements for details and the imposition of calculated optical corrections, may be most evident in the war memorials, the commercial buildings and the great cathedral design, but it is also present in the later houses. Like Le Corbusier, Lutyens developed his own modular scale and system of ratios, and in his houses he designed his roof planes at an inclination of 54.45 degrees so that, where they met at the corners, the slope would appear at an angle of 45 degrees. All this, together with his use of an 'Armature of Planes', was analysed in his son's memoir, published in 1942, which, Mary Lutyens later recorded, 'Father told me he could not understand a word of'.[61]

Once, when asked by a student, 'What is proportion?', Lutyens replied: 'God.' The architect Oliver Hill considered that 'In his conviction of the absolute values of beauty and truth, and in his identifying them with a system of mathematical proportion, Lutyens proved himself in an altogether different category from other architects'.[62] But proportional systems alone cannot make great architecture. Even if he believed in absolute beauty, Lutyens's ability to make beautiful shapes and to control planes in three dimensions in order to make a dynamic composition was surely intuitive and afterwards refined by and checked against mathematical systems. Hope Bagenal recalled that in 1932 Lutyens said that

'Proportion in architecture is what time and key are in music.' Walter George … says that the important thing is that Lutyens sketched by eye and checked his proportions on his modular scale. In one of his letters, Walter George gave me some quite incredible modular figures for the Viceroy's House, and then asked 'Is it worth it?' He, having contemplated the Viceroy's House ever since it was built, ought to know. His reply is Yes, and that, for me, is evidence.[63]

Even in his late, carefully composed Classical houses, determined by proportion and geometry, Lutyens's houses are essentially romantic creations; that is, their form was ultimately determined by a picture in the architect's mind – a three-dimensional composition. In that, he differed from his hero, Philip Webb, the design of whose

houses apparently began with the working out of the interior plan and were refined by the imperatives of craftsmanship and materials. Lutyens, as Goodhart-Rendel observed, possessed – like Wren – 'the sculptor's capacity of making beautiful shapes'. And this primary interest in shapes, in pure geometrical form, led him to do things which, perhaps, he ought not to have done. If architecture is more than image, the necessary intermediate stage between the architect's drawing and the published photograph, it should be designed to last. But Lutyens, it must be admitted, designed details that have caused both the original and subsequent owners problems. No ugly downpipes will be detected in the *Country Life* photographs, as the architect hated them and so did his best to avoid or conceal them – and it is difficult to clear blocked internal drainpipes. Similarly, Lutyens's concealed parapet gutters and valley gutters have also sometimes proved difficult and expensive to maintain. But he was far from the first, or the last, famous architect to commit such sins for the sake of cosmetic effect.

Today, many of Lutyens's houses may seem as contrived and inconvenient as the castles and palaces of Vanbrugh, but, like great houses of earlier centuries, they should be judged by different standards. So dramatic were the social and technological changes in just the first half of the twentieth century that A. S. G. Butler, writing fifty years ago in the years of austerity after the Second World War, looked back to the Edwardian period – the years of his youth – as if it was an incomprehensibly distant era, 'when much thought was given to the accommodation of staff, usually with a view rather to their reasonable comfort than to save labour. For there was plenty of labour,' he explained,

and devices for saving it were then in their infancy. And that is why … it is important to bear in mind that he belonged to the last years of the nineteenth century and the first years of the twentieth. It was not so much his concern to make these houses easy to live in as to create something very delightful to inhabit. Even in his latest designs, one can discover a certain inconvenience in the placing of rooms. The relation of a servants' hall to a kitchen, for instance. These were not always contiguous; and meals had to be carried some distance from one to the other. But there was a girl to do that. It was her job. One would not have sacrificed the symmetry of an exterior then, to save a few steps, as we should doubtless do now.[64]

The important point, however, was that even though social conditions may have changed, 'it does not alter the fact that these houses, when they were put up, did fulfil their purpose adequately'.

On the other hand, Goodhart-Rendel, who had been brought up at Chinthurst Hill, confessed that although 'that house continued for some years to be the romance of my life. From my mother's point of view it proved remarkably inconvenient … . Most of the bedrooms looked north up a steep hill, every fireplace smoked, the windows all let in the wet …'.[65] But that particular Lutyens house was an early, immature work. And, as Goodhart-Rendel admitted, 'Living in a Lutyens house may have its disadvantages, the offices are sometimes queer, you can't always see out of the windows, and there is an awful lot to dust and keep clean. I expect that the same was true of most fairy palaces, but the amenities of fairyland are worth a lot.'[66] 'Everything was unexpected, fantastic – and, of course, enormously expensive, which merely added a welcome *cachet* to ownership of "a Lutyens house".'[67]

In terms of services, Lutyens's Edwardian houses were not sophisticated – certainly not in comparison with contemporary American residences. Today this is evident in terms of heating and, above all, plumbing. The generous provision of bathrooms was still not regarded as a necessity in Britain, and Butler noted that at Overstrand Hall, for instance, 'there were ten bedrooms for the family and nine for the servants, with two bathrooms for all. Grey Walls had thirteen bedrooms and one bath. The proportion between bedrooms and bathrooms was 22 to 3 at Papillon Hall, 14 to 2 at Marsh Court, 13 to 3 at Little Thakeham and 6 to 1 at Deanery Garden.' Incorporating such small rooms with their associated

The 'writing room' on the staircase landing at Nashdom: the dial on the cartographic chimneypiece indicates wind direction.

plumbing can have a major impact on the appearance of a house, but Lutyens 'was saved a great deal of that complication in these early houses. He was saved as well the complexities of modern heating; for these residences belonged to a period when open fires were assumed to be the means of warming a house. A large number were lit by willing servants each morning; and, in the bedrooms, one washed in a tin bath. It was not unpleasant.'[68]

It is difficult to generalise about the character of Lutyens's interior spaces. Unlike Voysey, or Mackintosh, he had no single distinctive, personal style. Many of his grander reception rooms used the Classical language, with panelling and enriched plaster ceilings derived from historical models. Much of the interest comes from the shape of the space, and from the cleverness with which Lutyens treated doors, cupboards and, above all, the chimneypiece – all with

a close attention to detail. Perhaps the most characteristic and memorable of Lutyens's interior spaces are the most simple, where he relied on whitewashed walls and the texture of wood and stone, as at Lindisfarne Castle and in the corridors of Castle Drogo. Hussey suggested that Lutyens learned from Gertrude Jekyll, who had learned from Ruskin that 'Good whitewashed timber, and tapestry, are the proper walls of rooms in cold climates.'[69] Although he did occasionally design pieces of furniture, and created brilliantly original and witty light fittings, Lutyens did not usually conceive of rooms as complete, total works of art – as Mackintosh and Wright did – with every single element subordinate to a personal, totalitarian vision. As the *Country Life* photographs reveal, the furniture installed by his clients in his houses was often old and usually comfortable.

Where Lutyens did demonstrate originality and a personal style in his interiors was in the use of colour. Evidently he never forgot what he saw in Miss Cranston's tea-rooms in Glasgow and – when he was permitted to – he indulged in black walls and other striking effects using pure colour. In the double-height vaulted hall at Folly Farm, the walls were painted black and the woodwork white, with the Chinese Chippendale balconies lacquered red. This was an effect he had already tried out in his own drawing room at 29 Bloomsbury Square, where, in addition, the curtains were yellow and the floor painted green. Floors were important: at Lindisfarne Castle for Hudson, the oak floors were painted duck-egg blue or crimson with a thin layer of white dragged over. Hussey wrote that 'As a decorator, Lutyens was always austere, averse from rich colouring because form was his dominating interest and he mistrusted the sensuousness of colour effects. Colour, when used, must be strong and even, part of the architectural design and not overlaid and incidental.'[70]

In Bloomsbury Square the walls of the dining room were red and the floor green. Later, in the house in Mansfield Street, such effects were repeated and the furniture was always upholstered in black horsehair. His daughter Mary recalled that

Cushions and lampshades had to be as plain as possible (he could not abide frills, tassels, fringes or flounces), carpets on stairs and in bedrooms were of the dark grey hair-cord he had always favoured, specially made for him with narrow borders of black and yellow. (Pile carpets were another anathema.) The sitting room floor was painted red. These painted floors which were repeated in many of his houses in different colours needed innumerable coats of paint and varnish to prevent chipping but wore extremely well.[71]

Another unusual effect Lutyens occasionally tried was to paper the walls with pages of *The Times* newspaper (then printed on rather better paper) and varnish them.

Lutyens may not have been interested in the open plan which is such a conspicuous feature of Frank Lloyd Wright's contemporary

Right: *Queen Mary's Dolls' House in Lutyens's own drawing room in Mansfield Street, London, about to be removed to the British Empire Exhibition at Wembley in 1924.*

houses – his domestic spaces are usually enclosed – but that certainly does not mean he was not interested in spatial effects. As was appropriate in houses designed for weekend parties, Lutyens's corridors are usually generous spaces comfortable to linger in, while his staircases, in particular, are often spectacularly ingenious creations. In his honest and eloquent attempt to come to terms with an architect he knew he should respect but could not admire, Pevsner wrote how

Lutyens's handling of space has not in the past been sufficiently appreciated. The staircase at Little Thakeham is almost as ingenious with quite simple geometrical means as the staircases of the eighteenth century which we admire in Germany and Austria … . No wonder that Lutyens on his first journey to Italy got excited about the staircases of Genoa. 'The lavish space given away in staircases makes me sick with envy,' he wrote in 1909. If the architects of Genoa had seen the size of Lutyens's staircases at Delhi ten or twenty years later, the envy would have been theirs. England has never been particularly keen on ingenious or monumental stairs, and Lutyens's are among the finest she has produced.[72]

Hussey agreed, writing how, at Castle Drogo, the scale of the stairs 'is that of the great baroque palaces, with almost the grimness of Piranesi's imagination. The analogy is most apt to the head of the private stairs where the intersecting curves and receding vistas of domes is directly reminiscent of the Carceri.'[73] Sometimes Lutyens achieved his spatial effects with intricate structures of carefully pegged oak timbers; later, the gently curving treads might be of marble – with alternating black and white marble treads at Gledstone. Particularly in the later houses, like Viceroy's House and Middleton Park, the staircase halls, together with the all-important corridors, have a thrillingly monumental yet subtle grandeur never attained by Wright or Mackintosh.

Middleton Park, with its marble-lined and vaulted entrance corridor and extravagant lush bathroom for Lady Jersey, is Lutyens's grandest country house, and the last. It is one of the handful of new houses he designed between the two world wars, several of which were for old friends and clients, such as Hudson and Reginald McKenna, for whom he returned to his earlier vernacular manner. There were also Classical designs like Gledstone Hall, the pavilions at Tyringham Hall and that miniature curiosity, Queen Mary's Dolls' House – 'one of the few really dull things Lutyens has done', as John Summerson once rightly observed (anonymously)[74] – which, although serious as an architectural design, was not tied to a particular site nor subservient to any client's importunate demands. In addition there was the British Embassy in Washington, which is best regarded as a house since all Lutyens's great experience in planning for parties and social events, in separating the zones for guests and for owners, went into the complex planning of that sophisticated Americanised essay in the simple brick manner of Wren. But by the time it was built, Lutyens – by now knighted and an establishment figure: an unofficial 'Architect Laureate' – was best known as the architect of New Delhi, the designer of banks and commercial palaces, the creator of the Cenotaph and of poignant war

memorials and cemeteries in France, and the conceiver of a cathedral which, when completed, would vie not only with St Paul's but with St Peter's in Rome as well.

When, in 1913, Weaver published his compilation of *Country Life* articles and photographs of *Houses and Gardens by E. L. Lutyens*, he wrapped up almost all of the architect's domestic work that really mattered, for it was in those years just prior to the outbreak of war that his career changed direction. But there is one great exception to that generalisation, for Lutyens's greatest house was not completed until 1929. Unlike so many of his famous houses, this was a true Great House, a grand palatial residence at the heart of an important demesne which expressed the power and prestige of its occupant. It was a house in which all of Lutyens's sophisticated skill in planning for living and entertaining was brought into play, a house for banquets and parties on the most lavish scale, a house in which countless guests could be accommodated, a house with magical gardens attached, a house which was both a home and a palace – the greatest and yet most comfortable of palaces. Yet it was not built in England, or Scotland, or even in France but in the heat and dust of India. It is, of course, Viceroy's House at the heart of New Delhi.

As Robert Byron insisted, 'Viceroy's House is, above all else, a *house*'. And within that house, the four-storey wing planned expressly for the Viceroy and his family was designed like a complete country house.

The beauty of this building transcends the merely panoramic. The coloured and theatrical façade of Islam has been annexed to a more intellectual, three-dimensional tradition of solid form and exact proportion – the tradition of Europe. The result has been to create one of the great palaces of the world, and the only one erected within the last hundred years. Its architecture combines the grandeur of Bernini and the subtlety of Palladio with the colour, shade, and water of Mohammedan Asia. Its maker is Sir Edwin Lutyens, whom posterity will celebrate as the last of the humanists, and as an artist who expressed, in his medium, the splendour of a political idea.[75]

Lutyens worked harder and longer on Viceroy's House than on any other of his domestic commissions, and its appearance when new was recorded in a large number of specially taken *Country Life* photographs to accompany Byron's five-part eulogy of Lutyens's new city in the magazine. In the event, it was only occupied by a British Viceroy for a mere eighteen years, but it has now happily served as the official residence for the President of independent India for far longer. Viceroy's House has been condemned not so much for its imperial Classical architecture as for what it represented politically, although New Delhi was much admired by Le Corbusier when, later, he was building another new capital in India at Chandigarh. However, the architectural historian David Gebhard was, as an American, untroubled by post-imperial guilt and so could maintain that 'the Residency stands as a formidable argument: an argument for classical humanism, for man's ability to control and at the same time to accommodate himself to his physical and social

The entrance front of The Dormy House at Walton-on-the-Hill, Surrey (1906), a residential golf club for G. A. Riddell for the Walton Heath Golf Club.

environment – and against those planners and architects who, as ageing period pieces, still cling to the tenets of the "Modern Movement" in architecture.'[76]

Gebhard was writing in 1972 – in the *Sunday Times* colour magazine – when polemics in defence of Lutyens were necessary. After his death in 1944, Lutyens's reputation slowly declined as those Edwardian houses increasingly seemed an irrelevance, the products of a past, distant era. 'It is because plumbing and ventilating plants have come to be regarded as architectural functions that my father ... is dismissed by many of the younger generation of practitioners as an amateur,' complained Robert Lutyens in 1952.[77] The new orthodoxy about Lutyens had been expressed by Pevsner the year before when he wrote that 'his importance in the development of European architecture seems to me without any doubt less than, amongst his British contemporaries, Voysey's, and his originality less than Mackintosh's.'[78] Lutyens's 'importance', of course, depended on the direction a writer thought European architecture ought to be going in. Not everyone agreed with Pevsner, so, at the time of Lutyens's death, Albert Richardson could maintain that 'His

influence was widespread; it quickened American architects to fresh endeavour, and found followers at Hilversum, Stockholm and Dresden. The Englishman's love of a good-looking home and a decent fireside had raised the standard for such things throughout the world. Thus Lutyens became the embodiment of the domestic outlook of his time ...'.[79]

The centenary of the architect's birth in 1969 was the nadir, when it proved impossible to raise the funds to hold an exhibition at the Royal Academy (of which he had been president) and the *RIBA Journal* gave space to Alison and Peter Smithson to argue that Lutyens had perverted the course of modern English architecture. 'Lutyens was caught in the box of his time too tightly for it to be possible for my generation to think about his architecture without pain,' explained Peter Smithson. Three years earlier, in 1966, Robert Furneaux Jordan had condemned Lutyens by association in his Penguin guide to *Victorian Architecture*. 'Those famous dream houses,' he claimed,

... will remain as a most curious monument, not to a culture – for they are clean outside their time – but to one man. Like a dream they are unreal, and like a dream they have left not a wrack behind. They were Bernard Shaw's *Heartbreak House*. They were a gesture from a world where there were still impeccable maids in the Servants' Hall, glossy hunters in the

loose boxes, and Peter Pan in the nursery wing. It was all lily ponds, lavender walks and pot-pourri in a Surrey garden. It was also an architecture where the high-pitched roofs, textured stone and tiny casements served mainly to conceal, ever so charmingly, the whole apparatus of conspicuous waste. It all died, as it should have died, in August 1914.[80]

In fact, the answer to this specious dismissal had already been given by A. S. G. Butler in the *Lutyens Memorial* back in 1950 when he pointed out that 'because buildings planned for that society are unsuited to our present needs, that does not lessen their value as architecture. It is doubtful if anybody at all worships the old Greek gods to-day, yet we still applaud the designers of their temples.'[81]

As it happened, 1966 was the year which saw the beginnings of a Lutyens revival and it began on the other side of the Atlantic. In his influential tract, *Complexity and Contradiction in Architecture*, Robert Venturi (the future architect of the National Gallery extension in London) took Lutyens seriously both as a planner and because of the ambiguity and paradox in his work. Three years later, it was Venturi and his wife, Denise Scott Brown, who countered the 'condescending and irrelevant' articles by the Smithsons in the pages of the *RIBA Journal* and asked architects to 'uphold the Anglicisation of Classicism in the land of Wren, Hawksmoor, Vanbrugh, Archer, Adam and Soane ...'. And in that same centenary year in an American architectural journal, the South African-born architect Allan Greenberg published a study of the use of geometry and axes in Lutyens's house and garden plans and compared his work with that of both Wright and Le Corbusier.

Greenberg's formal, architectural approach was continued by Inskip in his 1979 analysis of the houses – the first new study of Lutyens's architecture published in Britain since the *Memorial* volumes. This was soon followed by the books on Lutyens by Daniel O'Neill and Roderick Gradidge, both of which were primarily concerned with the domestic architecture, and soon after came books and articles by Jane Brown, Margaret Richardson and Colin Amery, as well as by Robert Grant Irving, the American, on New Delhi. What, in fact, is so remarkable is that, whatever the ups and downs of Lutyens's reputation, the experience of his architecture has generated some extraordinarily fine and evocative pieces of writing by a wide range of architects and critics – hence the large number of pertinent quotations used unashamedly in this introduction.

Not that any of this controversy and re-evaluation ever affected the status of Lutyens's houses in the advertisement pages in *Country Life*, for they continued to be lived in and cherished much as before, albeit with necessary modernisation. Nor did it prevent the acquisition of two Lutyens houses (or, rather, castles: Lindisfarne and Drogo) by the National Trust in advance of a spoof prediction made by the *Architects' Journal* in 1935 that in 1990 an 'Early Lutyens House' would be 'bought for the Nation'. It is surely significant that only one Lutyens country house has been demolished – Papillon Hall

Left: *The east terrace at The Salutation at Sandwich, Kent: rectilinear precision in the manner of William and Mary with – most unusually for Lutyens – visible down-pipes.*

– and that was because it was haunted; the record of the legacy of poor Philip Webb is very different. (One London house, 42 Cheyne Walk, has also gone, but that was because it was really a country house in town and represented a most uneconomic use of the site, while Monkton was converted into a Surrealist fantasy in the 1930s by Christopher Nicholson for Edward James – apparently with Lutyens's blessing.) The principal danger to Lutyens's domestic architecture, indeed, is not so much neglect or unfashionability as money; the character of many of his finest houses has been altered in recent years by their increasingly affluent owners.

The 1970s saw a serious revival of interest in Lutyens's architecture, with Nicholas Taylor and Roderick Gradidge organising visits to many of the houses for the Victorian Society. All this reappraisal and new enthusiasm culminated in the Lutyens Exhibition held at the Hayward Gallery in London in the winter of 1981–82. Designed by the architect Piers Gough, this contained evocative re-creations of the different types of the architect's domestic interiors. The exhibition attracted a great deal of publicity and, despite a bad winter, some 80,000 visitors – many more than the Arts Council of Great Britain had expected.

At the time, the Lutyens Exhibition seemed to herald a renaissance of Lutyens studies and the re-establishment of Lutyens's status as a giant – *the* giant – in modern English architecture: the greatest British architect of the twentieth century. Yet, in retrospect, curiously enough, that exhibition seems to have been an end rather than a beginning, despite the subsequent formation of the Lutyens Trust and the acquisition by the Landmark Trust of one of his houses (Goddards). For while new books on his contemporaries Frank Lloyd Wright and Charles Rennie Mackintosh seem to come out almost every month, very little on Lutyens has been published since. More deserves to be: hence this present volume, exploiting the superb visual coverage of Lutyens's architecture made over a century by the photographers of *Country Life*, his consistently loyal ally.

Why this should be is puzzling. It may be that the Lutyens revival became associated with the now discredited rise of a vulgar commercial Post-Modernism in the 1980s, the decade of Margaret Thatcher, in which history was crudely and incompetently exploited as an alternative to the aridity of the Modern Movement. But it is more likely that what was Lutyens's strength, his very Englishness that was so admired by Weaver and Hussey and celebrated in the pages of *Country Life*, is now perceived as a liability. 'In his architecture he could catch the prevailing sentiment of a situation and reduce it to classic permanence,' John Summerson wrote in 1951. 'That is why he was so successful with his country houses, mostly built for people who had no particular discrimination in architecture but who were driven to recognise in his buildings the perfect embodiment of the sentiments they most cherished. In his houses Lutyens spoke – in brick and stone – for the inarticulate upper-class Englishman.'[82] The attitudes and aspirations of Lutyens's *milieu* are not now found sympathetic, perhaps. Wright and Mackintosh also designed houses for the wealthy, of course, but, rightly or wrongly, their clients are somehow regarded differently from the smug, wealthy Edwardians who gave Lutyens his opportunities. Yet again, Lutyens is found guilty by association.

This problem is exacerbated by the fact that Lutyens's most romantic, most sympathetic, most English and most typical houses remain firmly inaccessible to the public. Castle Drogo and Lindisfarne may be owned by the National Trust but they are distant and untypical, while it is not possible to visit, say, the great Surrey masterpieces like Orchards. It could do wonders for Lutyens's reputation if Deanery Garden or Marsh Court could be acquired to join Philip Webb's Standen in the National Trust's modern portfolio. The interested public could then experience Lutyens's domestic design as it can Mackintosh's at The Hill House, Helensburgh, or Wright's in Oak Park, Chicago.

Unfortunately, however, Lutyens – unlike Mackintosh or Wright – is also regarded as an establishment figure, associated with Empire, rather than as a tragic misunderstood genius, somehow ahead of his time (however mendacious and absurd such perceptions may be). Lutyens may well have had many of the conventional attitudes of a typical Englishman of his time and background but, as knighted architects go, he was in fact very far from being grand and pompous – indeed, he was notorious as a 'perennial *enfant terrible*'. Always accessible to and liked by the young, he remained shy and curiously inarticulate despite his fame. He expressed himself in drawings, sketches and caricatures, rather than in words – although he could write well enough when asked. In his manner and in his behaviour, he was not always conventional, as biographies and memoirs make clear, but behind all his jokes and psychological defences, Lutyens was an artist of profound seriousness. And he never, to the end, lost

that sense of wit, or the ability to design, as Goodhart-Rendel put it, 'the sudden unanalysable felicity that makes one catch one's breath'.

In reviewing the *Memorial* volumes, John Betjeman asked, 'What other architects have done so much work, with such haunting power to it and sudden humour?' And, after Lutyens's death, Goodhart-Rendel concluded that 'Whether by the reality of his buildings or by their photographic illustrations he gave to thousands of his generation happy dreams, and dreams were what they needed. He was a magician, a spell-binder ...'. Well, we still need our dreams. Lutyens's architecture still speaks to more recent generations without the means or even necessarily the aspiration to live in the sort of houses he created. Lutyens was an architect whose work appeals both to the intellect and to the heart. Rooted in the history of English domestic architecture, his brilliant reinterpretations can conjure up comfortable illusions of timeless rural domesticity, while thrilling the spectator with their ambiguities and paradoxes, their wit and essential humanity.

'My generation is – perhaps I ought to say was – a humanist generation,' Lutyens told the readers of *Country Life* in 1931. 'We believed that the measure of man's architecture was man, and that the rhythm of a building should correspond to the rhythms familiar in human life.' Tradition, for him, was not stultifying but liberating. 'By tradition,' he explained, 'I do not mean the unthinking repetition of antique forms – the hanging of Roman togas on Victorian towel-

Below: *Ground plans of Deanery Garden (1899) and Heathcote (1905), both printed to the same scale.*

Right: *The balconies, or sleeping porches, within the loggia at Monkton: a complex spatial arrangement which survived Edward James's Surrealist transformation in the 1930s.*

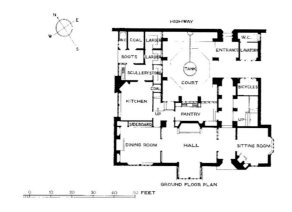

*The west front of Viceroy's House, seen from across Lutyens's formal Moghul
water garden in 1931.*

horses. Tradition to me consists in our inherited sense of structural
fitness, the evolution of rhythmic form by a synthesis of needs and
materials, the avoidance of arbitrary faults by the exercise of
common sense coupled with sensibility.'[83] And for no building type
was that more important than for the house – 'To be a home, the
house cannot be a machine,' he insisted in answer to Le Corbusier.[84]

In the longer run, perhaps Lutyens was not as influential as
Voysey, or Mackintosh, although, from the perspective of a new
century, that assessment may well change. Besides, architecture does
not necessarily have to be progressive, to lead anywhere, to be
important, or great – Hawksmoor's sublime, eclectic creations led
nowhere, after all. In his early work Lutyens owed much to Voysey,
and possibly even to Mackintosh. Nor did Lutyens and Mackintosh
diverge quite as much as is often supposed – the similarity in aim and
mood between the abstracted-Tudor of the celebrated west wing of
the Glasgow School of Art and the dramatic, faceted, almost contemporary east wing of Castle Drogo is tantalisingly clear. But perhaps
the most important comparisons are to be made with the domestic
work of his great American admirer, Frank Lloyd Wright. This is

not just in terms of planning, for the architecture of both celebrates
the supreme importance of controlling, dominating, inexorable horizontality. As Allan Greenberg observed, Wright was not influenced
by the English architect (or vice versa) but 'In Lutyens he found a
great mind grappling with related problems, and using similar orga-
nizational principles, but separated physically by an ocean, and intel-
lectually by another social system and the different terms by which
the principles were applied.'[85]

There is surely no harm in taking pleasure in romantic creations,
in the sheer beauty of materials and construction and in the suave
and inventive handling of historical styles that Lutyens's finest
houses offer. But it is also necessary to look beyond the oak beams
and Classical columns to the underlying geometry and that almost
miraculous sense of order and control combined with breathtaking
felicities that most of his creations demonstrate. There is so often an
essential rightness about his buildings, the result of what Goodhart-
Rendel called 'a rare subconscious perception of imponderables' that
might seem almost to approach the Platonic essence of Architecture
as pure form – perhaps that was what Herbert Baker recognised
when he observed that, even as a student, Lutyens 'seemed to know
by intuition some great truths of our art'. As Lutyens himself
insisted, 'Everything should have an air of inevitability'. This is

evident from first to last, in the unbroken continuity of the complex sweeps of roof at Middlefield or in the concave-chimneyed wings of Tigbourne; in the precise planes of granite at Drogo or in the continuity of the long walls of local rubble stone of, say, Orchards, with its terraced and walled gardens overlooking the Surrey hills; or in the dominating integrity of the horizontal cornice of Viceroy's House and those dynamic podia of battered red sandstone extending unbroken from its carefully considered basement wall planes rising above the red soil of Delhi.

In January 1931, Lutyens and his wife travelled out to India for the official opening of the new capital. He had invited Edward Hudson to go with him and all three stayed at Viceroy's House as the guests of Lord Irwin. Fortunately, Hudson took a *Country Life* photographer, Arthur Gill, with him so that his magazine could publish its favourite architect's greatest triumph. Lutyens's invitation to 'Huddy' was an appropriate gesture and this visit was the culmination of their relationship. The founder of *Country Life* was deeply impressed by what his old friend had achieved and Lady Emily Lutyens wrote home from New Delhi that Hudson was 'so moved that he can hardly keep from tears. He said to me yesterday "Poor old Christopher Wren could never have done this!"'[86] And Hudson was quite right.

* * *

The selection of houses that follows is (with the exception of Viceroy's House) in chronological order by the date of the design. It is intended to be representative of all phases of Lutyens's career but is partly determined by the material that survives in the archives of *Country Life*, which, to a considerable extent, reflects the taste of the original editor and his authors. Houses that were considered eccentric by Hudson or Weaver seem not to have been photographed. Other houses, however, are missing here for different reasons. Munstead Wood has been omitted because the original *Country Life* photographs have so often been published elsewhere. Orchards, on the other hand, is regrettably not covered in any detail because the original negatives of the views of the entrance courtyard, cloister and interior are missing, presumed lost or broken. Similarly, important and beautiful houses like Middlefield and The Salutation have had to be omitted as insufficient illustration survives of their interiors.

Lutyens's work at Hampstead Garden Suburb is not included, nor are his London houses, nor the town houses in New Delhi designed for the Nizam of Hyderabad and the Gaekwar of Baroda. Nor, alas, is there any record of the work Lutyens carried out in the 1920s for Victoria, Lady Sackville. Oliver Hill once recalled how he would draw Vita Sackville-West on the intriguing subject of her mother's association with Lutyens. On one occasion he told her of a spiritualist *séance* some time after Lutyens's death when he had asked the medium, who had known the architect, if she had seen him. '"Oh yes, he's here," came the reply. "What is he doing?" I asked. "Oh,

building." Vita thought for a brief moment; then, in her deep voice, she said: "God must be very rich."'[87]

Orchards is nevertheless the most serious omission in this compilation, but some of the surviving photographs of the house are reproduced in Jeremy Musson's volume on *The English Manor House*, in which New Place, Shedfield, and Temple Dinsley are also illustrated. Similarly, Lutyens's two castles in Ireland – Lambay and Howth – are covered in Seán O'Reilly's collection of *Irish Houses and Gardens*. Deanery Garden has also been illustrated in Michael Hall's pioneering volume on *The English Country House*, but as it was so important to Lutyens and to Edward Hudson and to his magazine, repetition here is surely justified. (Lutyens's work inside Hudson's house in Queen Anne's Gate is discussed by John Cornforth in his volume on *London Interiors*.) In understanding any house, and particularly those by Lutyens, study of the ground plan is essential, but it has not been possible to reproduce these within the format of this book; the interested reader is therefore referred to Weaver's and other studies of Lutyens's houses.

Most of the houses illustrated here were recorded soon after they were built – usually by Charles Latham in the early days or by A. E. Henson after the Great War. The principal exception is Le Bois des Moutiers, originally ignored by *Country Life* but at last published in 1981, having been photographed by Alex Starkey. A majority of the photographs, however, show the houses as their architect intended they should look: mellow and yet monumental, fitting into the soft English landscape and enhanced by the luxuriant state of their gardens – planted, of course, according to the recommendations of Miss Jekyll. Inside, there is the old oak furniture, the pewter and china, the carpets and tapestries favoured by their original owners (even if sometimes rearranged by the photographer). These photographs, therefore, show Lutyens's houses performing as they were designed to perform, before the kitchens were modernised, the gardens simplified and the interiors compromised to accord with modern taste. Indeed, several of them have since suffered more from improvement than they would have done from neglect. Contemplating the original photographs of Hudson's Deanery Garden is particularly poignant, as that realised ideal of *Country Life* has, in recent decades, been successively spoiled by the untutored arrogance of great wealth.

Above all, these photographs depict some of the loveliest houses ever raised in England. Photographs may mislead or distort – although nothing like as much as an architect's seductive drawings – but they also give reality to the dreams of their time. *Country Life* illustrated dreams: timeless dreams of rural English domesticity, for most readers unattainable, and yet real. Some of these visions were old, but some were new. And of the new houses presented in beautiful photographs, the most distinguished and most desirable were those designed by the magazine's first and greatest star, Edwin Lutyens – an architect of rare genius and humanity for whom 'Architecture, with its love and passion, begins where function ends'.

ONE

CROOKSBURY

'… I got a house to build at nineteen, and I've been building them ever since …' Lutyens told the Architectural Association in 1920. 'It was great fun that first house. I advise everyone to build a house at nineteen. It's such good practice.'[88] Perhaps he was thinking of Crooksbury, his first house, although he was in fact twenty years old when he designed it. Crooksbury was also the first of his houses to be published in *Country Life*. Eventually the result of three building campaigns, this house near Farnham, Surrey, is not a coherent whole, but it illustrates the development of the architect's skills and the successive phases of his domestic manner. And if the first phase gives no hint of the promise of the designer of New Delhi and the Cenotaph, the second phase certainly did.

Crooksbury was commissioned from the very young and ambitious architect in 1889 by a family friend, Arthur Chapman, a director of Piggot, Chapman & Co., exporters of Calcutta, who had returned home from India and, in 1902, achieved his ambition of retiring from business to be a country gentleman and hunt.

When Lutyens wrote in 1910 that 'I can't help being jealous of Chippy who has no living to make and all his spare time!', his wife rebuked him, replying: 'I think it naughty of you to be jealous … when you remember the years he has spent in working far away in India without wife or home and every penny of his money is self made.'[89] Liberal, kind and always helpful, particularly to his adored Lady Emily whom he accompanied to political meetings, Chapman was also responsible for Lutyens being asked to design the Liberal Club in nearby Farnham.

Preceding pages (left): *The south end of the east wing of Crooksbury, Surrey, as transformed by Lutyens in 1914 into roughcast Tudor.*
(right): *The original half-timbered and tile-hung house, as designed by the young Lutyens in 1889 and seen from the entrance to the forecourt.*

Left: *A transformation* – (below): *the east wing as first built in 1898.*
(above): *the same elevation after being transformed by Lutyens in 1914; the stables of 1902 can be seen beyond.*

Above: *The Fig Court with its pergola, created in 1898 – the original house is to the left; the new wing to the right.*

The small half-timbered and tile-hung house that Lutyens first built in 1890 owed much to Ernest George, whose office he had just left, as well as to the Surrey houses of Norman Shaw. It is not remarkable. In 1898, Chapman asked Lutyens to double his house in size. As with other of his houses that he enlarged, he did so in a deliberately different – later – style. A new east wing was built some way from the original house, and this was an essay in his Classical 'Wrennaissance' manner. The principal façade was of red brick, with slightly projecting symmetrical wings facing the gardens, and had eight bays of windows of a seventeenth-century character, and a pitched-tiled roof rose behind a straight parapet. The only element which broke the precise symmetry was the pedimented and rusticated doorcase, which was placed off centre to gain access to a corridor between the new drawing and dining rooms which connected with the older part of the house.

Christopher Hussey later explained that this addition 'took the form of a brick William-and-Mary wing such as might have been added two centuries later to a yeoman's hall … the source of it was still homely – the houses of Surrey farmers who had prospered under the Corn Laws'. Between the two blocks, Lutyens designed the Fig Court, with tile-hung walls to bridge the transition. Here he created a deep pergola and an interesting balcony with metal supports to the roof above which, to judge by the original *Country Life* photographs, had something of the Art Nouveau character of his contemporary work elsewhere. Finally, in 1902, a stable block was completed – symmetrical, with generous pitched roofs below a Classical cupola.

In 1953, the Farnham architect Harold Falkner wrote to Christopher Hussey commenting that while the original house 'was not to my mind up to the average production of an ex-pupil of a good office', when Chapman decided to enlarge it 'Lutyens produced a building which was a revelation. It had not the least relation to the existing and turned its back on it. It foreshadowed everything that Lutyens was to become, A perfect mastery of materials, a most ingenious plan … and a serene front looking out on the stone paved terrace and garden, prophetic of all that [Lutyens and Gertrude Jekyll] afterwards did.'[90]

Chapman's wife Agnes died in 1906. As Falkner put it, 'The light had gone out for Chippy, he sold the house and retired to Whitehall Court, took various chairmanships of public bodies, a knighthood, obscurity and died. The new owner insisted in destroying the garden wing of Crooksbury, and Lutyens, who as usual wanted money, quarter-timbered it. It must have been about the bitterest pill any so sensitive a person ever swallowed.' This was T. E. Briggs, for whom, in 1914, Lutyens designed an unsatisfactory essay in streamlined-'olde-worlde-oaky'-Tudor which did not even harmonise with his original Ernest-Georgian-Tudor. He replaced red brick with roughcast, substituted bands of timber-framed windows for those Wren might have installed, and replaced the parapet by deep eaves. The Fig Court was also simplified, and spoiled. As Hussey commented, 'if he would not do it, somebody else would, so rather than let alien hands dismember his first-born, he hardened his heart and plunged in the adze himself.' Afterwards, Lutyens could never bear to visit the house again, as 'It has too many ghosts'. Perhaps he was thinking of this when, in 1932, he was asked what he considered his worst architectural crime and replied, 'A certain house built in Surrey. It was sold to a man who wanted me, I am glad to say, to alter it. I altered it beyond all recognition.'[91]

Gertrude Jekyll may have written the article when Crooksbury was illustrated in *Country Life* for 15 September 1900. The revamped east front and the stables were presumably photographed when Christopher Hussey wrote up the house again in the issues for 6 and 13 October 1944.

The drawing room with its deep inglenook fireplace in the original 1889 house, but after a later remodelling.

TWO

SULLINGSTEAD

Sullingstead was built at the same time as Gertrude Jekyll's Munstead Wood, not so far away. The house is one of Lutyens's
first mature works in the romantic vernacular manner so appropriate in Surrey, and the sophistication of the properly pegged half-
timbering forming the entrance front and of the sweeps of tile-hung wall facing the garden show that he had nothing more to learn from
his old master Ernest George – or from the houses of the great Norman Shaw.

Sullingstead (now known as High Hascombe) at Hascombe was built in 1896–97 for the lawyer Charles Arthur Cook,
later Sir Charles Cook, Chief Charity Commissioner. The site was awkward and confined, sloping down from north to south,
so that the house is approached on foot down steps from a porch raised up on the boundary wall to the north.

The Classical orders make an early appearance in this porch in the shape of stubby Tuscan columns below the hipped roof. The entrance front is a study in massive oak-timber construction relieved by small leaded-light windows. The principal rooms face south, and the ground-floor walls and windows are recessed below a bold run of tile-hanging on the first floor with an exaggerated flare at the base. And on this floor Lutyens indulged in that would-be proto-modernist feature of a timber-framed window wrapping around a corner.

In 1903, Lutyens was asked to add a music room to the left of the garden front, and he made this look distinct by adopting a style of apparently later date, that is, Georgian, in brick and stone rather than tile, and with big sash windows with shutters. But the horizontal lines of the composition continue through and when the music room turns the corner, weather-boarded gables replace the hipped roof. As Lawrence Weaver observed, 'in the result the two distinct motifs of design are mingled so subtly and yet so rightly that the whole house maintains its unity'.

Preceding pages (left): *The tile-hung garden front of Sullingstead seen from the east, with the music room added a little later by Lutyens on the left.*
(right): *The south-facing garden front; in the foreground is the music room, added in 1903 in a contrasting style.*

Left: *The half-timbered entrance front seen from the high-level porch by the road with its squat, white-painted Tuscan columns.*

Above: *The kitchen wing to the east of the main garden front.*

Weaver would seem to have preferred the rustic Georgian addition at Sullingstead to the original house, for many similar early Lutyens houses in the same picturesque vernacular style were omitted from his 1913 *Country Life* book on *Houses and Gardens by E. L. Lutyens*. The tile-hung gables, the overhanging upper storey and – above all – those interesting corner windows were all used at that very inventive house, Berry Down in Hampshire, at about the same time, but there the composition was much too eccentric to be shown to *Country Life* readers – especially as the roughcast entrance front might have reminded them of the cranky work of architects like Voysey and Baillie-Scott. To find a photograph of Berry Down, one must look at the issue of *The Studio* for January 1909; again – rightly or wrongly – the way we still see Lutyens's work is still affected by the editorial policy of *Country Life* in the early days.

Sullingstead first seems to have been photographed by *Country Life* for the 1913 book – Weaver had to include *some* of Lutyens's early work, after all.

Left: *The entrance front seen from the west through the gate in the garden wall.*

Above: *The interior of the music room with its Classical chimneypiece – the door on the right leads into a store cupboard piled up with logs.*

THREE

FULBROOK HOUSE

Fulbrook House was a product of a period of intense activity in Lutyens's early career and one of a group of richly inventive houses
within the Surrey vernacular tradition that established his reputation. Perhaps, however, he put too much into the design,
tried out too many new and unresolved ideas, for while this house has delighted many commentators, it has provoked severe criticism
from some of Lutyens's most ardent admirers.

For Lawrence Weaver, 'Too many techniques are employed at once … Also in the mass and outline of the house there is a somewhat too
vigorous pursuit of the picturesque'. While as far as Christopher Hussey was concerned, 'The design, an exuberant outcome of
Munstead undertaken in the first flush of his excitement following his betrothal, is the worst he ever made'. But as Roderick Gradidge –
an enthusiast for the house who added a swimming-pool wing to it in 1974 – has observed very pertinently, 'Those who find Lutyens
at his most exciting when he is at his blandest – shall we say at Gledstone – will find little to praise at Fulbrook'.[92]

Jane Brown considers that 'Lutyens's happiest Surrey house – in human terms – is Fulbrook at Elstead, built in exciting days',[93] and, thanks to her, the accounts and specification of works and other documents have been published so that we know more about the building of this Lutyens house than any other. The first sketch designs were made towards the end of 1896, the full drawings were ready in February 1897, a tender of £6,840 was accepted at the end of March and the roof was on by December. However, work was dragging on in the autumn of 1898 and at the end of the year there were arguments over disputed extras – the main one being the entrance and stables costing about £2,000. The clients moved in to their house in the spring of 1899 and the final cost was £9,849. 14s.3d, including the architect's fee of £458.12s.6d but excluding the cost of the land, which was £2,500.

Like Munstead Wood and Orchards, Fulbrook was built of the local Bargate stone, with massive chimneys of red brick. The builders were Badcock and Maxey, the former name being that of the architect E. Baynes Badcock, who actually became Lutyens's business partner for a short and unhappy period. The client was Gerard Dorrien Streatfield, a gentleman archaeologist and ornithologist from Chiddingstone who had a passion for cricket.

His wife, Ida, was the daughter of Richard Henry Combe, who had built nearby Pierrepont, designed by Norman Shaw twenty years earlier. Mrs Streatfield had her own firm ideas about the sort of house she wanted; modern-minded, with an unusual interest in motor cars, she was photographed sitting in her 4½-horsepower *Locomobile* outside her new house for *The Car Illustrated* magazine for 9 July 1902 (Fulbrook was published in *Country Life* for 31 January 1903).

The plan is awkward: an Elizabethan 'E' plan is given one enlarged end wing to form the principal south front overlooking a terrace and sloping gardens. The east, entrance front has a central entrance, but the southern wing is larger and the picturesque asymmetry is enhanced by a tile-hung turret (containing an extra

Preceding pages (left): A detail of the entrance front of Fulbrook House – the tile-hung turret, which contains an extra lavatory, was a genuine afterthought. (right): The entrance elevation seen from the top of the formal gardens which rise to the west of the house.

Above: The hall, with its Classical fireplace with flanking glazed cupboards in an Ionic apse, and the principal staircase beyond.

Right: The bottom of the main staircase, where Lutyens played games with semicircular arches placed both vertically and horizontally.

lavatory) which was a genuine afterthought. It is the south front which has particularly worried Lutyens's admirers. A continuous hipped roof between protecting gables sails over a deep, asymmetrically placed recess, with chamfered corners within which timber bedroom balconies emerge on the first floor. And this massive roof is apparently supported on rather flimsy, curved timber braces – a feature which, Roderick Gradidge argues, comes from Kentish Wealden cottages illustrated in Ralph Nevill's 1889 book on *Old Cottage and Domestic Architecture in South-West Surrey*. Weaver was disturbed by this 'loggia': 'It is delightful, but at what a cost of structural honesty … . To what strange shifts Sir Edwin was put by way of ironwork concealed in the roof I do not know, but they must have been queer and considerable. It is not as though the amiable fraud were convincing …'. But Gradidge insists that there is no steel up there and that the internal structure is all of timber.

Fulbrook House shows Lutyens playing accomplished games with the Picturesque vernacular language of gables, timber and tile-hanging, which Ida Streatfield knew well from her childhood home. He also played games inside, where the style is very different. The interior is remarkable because it is Classical for the first time in Lutyens's work. An Ionic order appears in the main hall. And then Lutyens experimented with the details: the semicircular arches flanking the bottom of the staircase support another semicircle laid flat to make the edge of the upper floor level. Such were the beginnings of Lutyens's inventive Mannerism in the Classical language.

The south front, with its disturbing overhanging roof above the recessed balconies ostensibly supported by the curved timber brackets.

FOUR

LE BOIS DES MOUTIERS

Le Bois des Moutiers at Varengeville-sur-Mer is one of Lutyens's few houses outside Britain and one of a handful of houses (including Berry Down, The Pleasaunce at Overstrand and The Ferry Inn at Rosneath) in which he experimented with forms and details that make them comparable with the more unusual Arts and Crafts designs in England and the Art Nouveau of Scotland and the Continent. These houses were ignored by *Country Life* at the time and this most remarkable house in Normandy was only published in the issues of 21 and 28 May 1981, with new photographs by Alex Starkey to accompany the articles by Clive Aslet.

The Anglophile client, Guillaume Mallet, came from a French Protestant banking family; his wife, Adélaïde Grunelius, was half-German, had a similar banking background, and knew Lady Emily Lutyens's aunt, Mrs Earle, formerly Theresa Villiers and the author of *Pot-pourri from a Surrey Garden.*

Lutyens first met the Mallets in Paris in 1898 after he had been appointed to design the British pavilion at the 1900 Exposition Universelle, and he was asked to enlarge and remodel a house they had bought at the fashionable Normandy resort near Dieppe. Lutyens's fee was £186 on an agreed budget of 93,000 francs.

Working abroad seemed to present no difficulties. 'Such a day of it yesterday,' Lutyens wrote to his wife in August 1898. 'Seven French builders, the different trades. Oh such talking – such tremendous demonstrations and the excitement at times beyond all description. From 9 a.m. till 7.00 p.m. did this war (or Wagnerian Opera) of tongues cleave the air. You would have laughed.' And, two months later, 'Made a French joke with *immense* success with the French mason. He wanted to do something in stone which belonged to a wood construction, so I said in indignation it was pour bois! And added "Mais pas pour boire!" Great fits and I was pleased. M. Riche, the entrepreneur and bricklayer, is intelligent and a good sort of keen energetic man – very fond of practical demonstrations and drawing pictures upon the floor – a game at which I excel too.'[94] But surviving correspondence indicates that British craftsmen were also sent over, and that Guillaume Mallet was particularly impressed by the work of the plumbers. And Lutyens's tiresome partner Badcock occasionally visited the site.

Buried inside Le Bois des Moutiers is the original, rectangular brick house facing the view towards the sea. Lutyens extended it at both ends, added a wing to the south containing the entrance and staircase, and roughcast whatever was left exposed. To the west Lutyens built a large, double-height music room with a gallery and a decorative plaster ceiling by George Bankart. This magnificent room was lit by a giant window facing north towards the sea, with two tall, thin oriels rippling in a grid of small panes. To the east, Lutyens added service accommodation to make one of the most exciting and unusual elevations he ever designed. It is a composition in two planes. Flanking a massive blank chimneybreast are two wings whose tile-hung gables rise above a concave dropped cornice, while in the centre, above a circular window, the lintel of a wider rectangular window is formed by massive voussoir stones and a keystone. Here is a creative experiment in form, a piece of inventive Mannerism designed several years before Lutyens took up the language of Palladio and Sanmicheli in earnest.

In front of this astonishing side elevation are some of the roughcast walls, topped by a little tiled roof and occasionally pierced by arched openings with radiating 'voussoirs' of tiles, which divide up the surrounding area into a series of enchanting gardens or 'green rooms'. Lutyens redesigned the approach to the house, replacing the former diagonal drive with a direct route to the entrance at right angles to the house. A little later, in 1904, Gertude Jekyll sent over a plan for a spring shrub garden.

Everywhere at Le Bois des Moutiers the forms and details are engagingly eccentric. As the French writer Emmanuel Ducamp observes, Lutyens created a cleverly asymmetrical house 'which relates neither to the English vernacular style he was developing in England at the same time nor to the so-called *style normand* in vogue around Dieppe and Deauville during the Belle Epoque'.[95] Tiny protecting oriels sit below the eaves at the corners, while longer oriels distinguish the entrance wing, with its open round arches. Such oriels come from Norman Shaw but via such inventive designers as Arthur Heygate Mackmurdo and, possibly, Charles Rennie Mackintosh. As Christopher Hussey wrote, 'In the design of Le Bois des Moutiers at Varengeville, whether deriving from Paris or Glasgow, occurs one of the rare instances in his work of the influence of nouveau art modernism'. Glasgow is the more likely. The Mallets were conspicuous for their admiration for the English Arts and Crafts and their house contained furniture by Ambrose Heal, Morris chairs, a library table designed by W. R. Lethaby, fabrics by Walter Crane, plaster reliefs on the bedroom doors and a fireback by Robert Anning Bell and – its glory – a Morris tapestry of *The Adoration of the Magi* by Burne-Jones, woven for the house in 1904.

A decade later, Lutyens was asked by the Mallets to design another house in Varengeville, known as La Maison des Communes. Smaller than Le Bois des Moutiers, it is very different in style: more formal, with a mansard roof, and built of flint and brick in a decorative pattern. But what makes the house distinctive is its butterfly plan, with three wings radiating from the centre.

Preceding pages (left): *Le Bois des Moutiers seen from the north across the informal garden in 1981, with Lutyens's music room in the foreground.*
(right): *The south front of the music room seen across one of the 'green rooms' enclosed by Lutyens's tile-roofed walls.*

Above: *The projecting wing with its curious corner oriels added by Lutyens on the south side to contain a new entrance and the staircase.*

Right: *The extraordinary new east elevation created by Lutyens – perverse, brilliant and thrilling: an early essay in ambiguity and Mannerism.*

This house was under construction in 1909. That year both Lutyens and his wife stayed at Varengeville. It was a fateful visit: the Mallets were both Theosophists and Lady Emily was at first intrigued, lent a book of lectures by Annie Besant, and then hooked.

Theosophy soon created a great divide between Emily and Edwin Lutyens; in 1911 she was lent Les Communes by the Mallets and took Krishnamurti and his brother as well as her children to stay. Lady Emily was there again in 1913 and it was at Varengeville that summer that she was put on probation by her chosen Master, Kuthumi, and so took her first step on the Path. She was a member of the inner Esoteric School within the Theosophical Society and 'One of the requirements for discipleship was absolute physical as well as mental purity,' Mary Lutyens later explained, so 'even conjugal sex was taboo for pupils of the Master. Emily had discovered that the Mallets, who were both pupils, now had a *mariage blanc* after producing two children. This strengthened her in the resolve she had already made to break off sexual relations with Ned, although it was to be another year before she found the courage to tell him so ...'.[96]

Above: *The interior of the music room with the gallery on the south side, supported on eccentric brackets.*

Right: *The double-height music room with its elaborate plaster ceiling and huge oriel window, seen from the gallery in 1981.*

FIVE

GODDARDS

Goddards is one of Lutyens's loveliest houses: an inventive exemplar of Arts and Crafts ideals, beautifully made and with
an enchanting courtyard garden designed in collaboration with Gertrude Jekyll. Yet it was not originally built as a house; rather, it was
designed as a holiday 'Home of Rest' for 'ladies of small means' – governesses, nurses and others deserving of rest in idyllic countryside away from the bustle and dirt of London. Only in 1910 did Lutyens return to extend the building and convert it into a more
conventional family home. The philanthropic client was a Scot, Frederick James Mirrielees, who had been brought up to run the family
business, Muir & Mirrielees, which ran a department store in Moscow. He had married another Scot, Margaret Currie, one of the
daughters of Donald Currie MP, the owner of the Castle Steamship Company. One of Currie's conditions for agreeing to the marriage was
that Mirrielees should come and work for what became the Union Castle Line. Currie was himself an interesting architectural patron,
having commissioned the brilliant but short-lived architect James Maclaren to build both harled farm buildings and cottages on
his Glenlyon estate in Perthshire and a remarkable pair of brick houses in Palace Court, Bayswater – the former buildings having a
profound influence on the young Mackintosh.

Something of the Scottish character of Maclaren's work is evident at Goddards.

Mirrielees had built a house at Abinger Common near Dorking designed by another Scottish architect, William Flockhart, where Gertrude Jekyll helped with the gardens. Soon Lutyens was introduced. 'Went over yesterday to Mirrielees,' he reported in September 1898. 'He wants to build a little house or rather two cottages with a common room behind them to lend poor people, sick children Etc etc with a court. He don't know what he wants to spend but wishes to do it well, He is very rich & it all seems ideal as regards conditions under which the work will be done & I am

Preceding pages (left): *The interior of the skittle alley in the south wing of Goddards, Surrey: note the demountable section of the runnel for returning balls where it crosses the door.*
(right): *The east-facing gabled entrance front of the house, seen from the road: only the front door to the left disturbs the symmetry.*

Left: *The new end to the north wing added by Lutyens in 1910, with its carefully modelled chimney-stack containing an inglenook fireplace for the ground-floor dining room.*

Below: *The common room, or hall, photographed when the house was a home of rest; the hood of the fireplace plays on the theme of coves and arches in red brick.*

very happy and keen about it.'[97] Mirrielees, whom Jane Brown describes as 'perhaps the kindest and most gentlemanly of all Lutyens's early patrons', had bought another site at Abinger Common, of 7 acres, for his venture. The work was carried out by Harrisons of Abinger during 1899.

Goddards is the first of Lutyens's houses which is (almost) symmetrical. Towards the boundary wall, the east entrance elevation presents a simple frontage with twin gables flanked by tall brick chimneys. On the opposite side, however, facing the garden, two wings extend from the central range containing the hall. These splay outwards at an angle, on a 'butterfly' plan, enclosing a courtyard garden and allowing it to catch the afternoon sun. Lutyens revelled in the variety of building materials at Goddards. The roofs are of tile, with – unusually – courses of Horsham stone slates at a lower level. The windows have brick mullions and surrounds, with stone transoms. Otherwise the walls are roughcast, and on the flanking elevations the use of tapering buttresses is reminiscent of Voysey's work. Inside, the oak beams carrying the roof of the original communal hall are supported on curved, timber brackets, while the dominant chimneypiece plays games with brick arches and coves. The ground floor of the south wing is occupied

by a skittle alley, with the inclined trough for returning balls made dismountable where it runs across the outside door.

In August 1901, Lutyens wrote to his wife that he 'Went down to Goddards and went over the place. It seems very successful & the intimates love it & invariably weep when they leave it which is comforting. Mirrielees seems very happy with it too. Besides Miss Marryat or Mariot the custodian there are 3 nurses & 2 old governesses resting there & another nurse coming tomorrow … . We all played a game of skittles in my alley! I like using things I make.'[98] Shortly afterwards, the house was briefly used as a convalescent home for soldiers returned from the war in South Africa. In 1901, Lutyens tried to persuade Mirrielees to enlarge Goddards on the model of St Mary's Hospital, the almshouse at Chichester, but in vain.

As designed in 1898, Goddards was intended for use only in the summer and so had no bathrooms. In 1910, Mirrielees asked Lutyens to alter it to make a house for his son Donald and his wife. Both wings were extended to make a study and library at the end of the south wing and a dining room in the north wing, with a new bedroom above each. At the end of each of these new ground-floor rooms is a large inglenook fireplace, expressed externally by a massive chimneybreast topped by twin-angled brick chimneys.

These new wing ends are superb examples of Lutyens's handling of form, with the wall planes stepped back by slated slopes, first on the outer walls, then on the end wall as the building rises – a system of sculpting mass similar to that employed on the Cenotaph a decade later.

Goddards was illustrated in *Country Life* on 30 January 1904, but new photographs showing the alterations and additions were taken for Weaver's 1913 book. In 1991, Goddards was given to the Lutyens Trust by Bill and Noeline Hall, who had cared for the house lovingly, in memory of their son Lee; in 1996, it was transferred to the Landmark Trust. It is therefore the only example of Lutyens's early romantic vernacular work which is sometimes open to the public.

Above: *The west-facing courtyard after both splayed wings were extended by Lutyens in 1910; the formal garden lies behind the hedge.*

Right: *The well in the courtyard garden photographed before the windows were enlarged in 1910 to make the common room into a drawing room.*

SIX

OVERSTRAND HALL

North Norfolk was a fashionable place to holiday at the end of Victoria's reign when Cromer grew into a popular resort, with big, exuberant red-brick hotels designed by George Skipper, the Norwich architect. 'Between 1880 and 1914 Cromer became the place to go,' Mark Girouard later explained in *Country Life*. 'Rich upper and upper middle class ladies of those days liked to be what was called "artistic"; and it became fashionable for these smart artistic ladies to take or to send their families to Cromer for the summer. On its broad beaches well-born babies were taken for trips in little goat-drawn carts and thoroughly "nice" Kate-Greenaway-looking children in jerseys and straw hats paddled and made castles in the sand. Kate Greenaway herself was likely to be there …'.[99]

Even the Empress Elizabeth of Austria paid a visit, in 1887, while Edward VII, when Prince of Wales, became patron of the Royal Cromer Yacht Club. This was because he was a friend of Lord Suffield, who, according to legend, set fire to nearby Gunton Hall rather than continue to bear the expense of entertaining that large royal sybarite.

The Norfolk coast either side of Cromer became known as 'Poppyland' after the eponymous book published by Clement Scott, and summer houses sprang up along its length. Several are remarkable Arts and Crafts creations, made of local materials and often built on the splayed 'butterfly' plan which Lutyens had used at Goddards. There was Happisburgh Manor designed by Detmar Blow and Home Place at Holt by E. S. Prior. Lutyens added two to this list and planned two more. The two that were built are at Overstrand, near Cromer, which was developed by Lord Suffield after 1888, and the more successful by far is Overstrand Hall. It is a curious and experimental design, mixing the Tudor with the Classical and combining symmetrical elevations in a picturesque manner, all carried out in a rich mixture of building materials.

The client was the banker Charles Mills, a partner in Glynn Mills, Currie & Co., who had become the second Lord Hillingdon in 1898; his wife, Alice Harbord, was the daughter of Lord Suffield. 'I like Lord H. awfully,' Lutyens reported to his wife in September 1899, '... he likes all I like and looks at many things from the same point of view', which was surely fortunate. 'Saw Lord and Lady Battersea,' Lutyens wrote on the way back from Cromer the preceding October, '– both kind. Lord B. wants to alter more and is in a spoiling mood. The Curzons were there but I weren't introduced. Lord Hillingdon seems pleased and the house will be good and a jolly one to do. I don't think Lord Battersea quite likes the idea of a beautiful neighbour.'[100]

That was scarcely surprising: Lutyens's work for him was The Pleasaunce at Overstrand, which was already building. Lord Battersea had declined to let his architect build afresh but insisted that he enlarge and adapt two existing villas on the site which he had bought in 1888. The result is one of the architect's oddest houses: full of clever tricks and eccentricities and touches of Art Nouveau but, as an overall composition, a disaster. Battersea was the former Liberal MP and aesthete Cyril Flower; his wife, Constance, was the daughter of Sir Anthony Rothschild and she later recalled how, 'On my yearly arrivals ... I would expect to be greeted by some novelty, of which I was not always prepared to be an enthusiastic admirer; thus the first impression of the clock tower and of the cloisters was not a favourable one. Yet now I am quite attached to the tower ... . On one occasion I was startled by the sight of some masons constructing a high brick wall to the balcony of the window in my sitting room, which would effectually have

shut out the view from my seat in my favourite corner. I indignantly began to remonstrate, and in spite of Sir Edwin Lutyens's orders, threw the bricks down to the terrace, to the ill-concealed amusement of the workmen.'[101] No wonder The Pleasaunce is a confusing and confused building.

As for Overstrand Hall, Lord Hillingdon's house nearby, it was an entirely new build and designed around a courtyard. The house was planned for movement through the external and internal spaces, and, as A. S. G. Butler observed, 'the official access from the Porch to the Hall is quite an enterprise for a visitor. He leaves the shelter of the Porch, crosses the Court, circumnavigates a fountain and mounts one or other of the twin flights of curved steps to the front door. This admits him to a Vestibule, 45 feet long, running at right angles across his path; and he is faced by a fireplace in an inviting alcove. He resists that and, by turning twice to the right, he reaches ultimately the door to the Hall at the south end of the Vestibule.'[102]

In the design, Lutyens explored a series of symmetries, inside and out. The external south and east elevations are symmetrical, the east having a strange duality with two pairs of double arches and a central chimney-stack. Each of these fronts is terminated by a projecting deep oriel bay with a tile-hung gable placed well behind a stepped horizontal parapet – the Tudor style is reminiscent of the later work of Shaw but the whole composition has a strong horizontality characteristic of Lutyens. Half-timber appears on the south elevation and in the entrance passageway; the walls are otherwise of rough local flint relieved with bands of patterned tile, and with red brick used as quoins at the corners and for the window surrounds and mullions.

Inside, the staircase and hall are of properly pegged timbers, but round Classical arches appear to make loggias both inside the courtyard and facing the gardens. Most remarkable of all is the

Preceding pages (left): *The central Fountain Court at Overstrand Hall, seen through the deconstructed Classical arch at the end of the entrance passage.* (right): *The entrance front seen from the south-west: the arch on the right leads to the arch into the Fountain Court.*

Above: *The fireplace in the main hall: one of the most extraordinary Lutyens ever designed, a Mannerist composition of niches, concavities and attenuated corbel brackets.*

Right: *The principal staircase, constructed of properly pegged oak timbers with a landing behind a semi-transparent half-timbered screen.*

highly inventive and sculptural hall fireplace – one of the most remarkable Lutyens ever designed – and the inner entrance 'skeleton' arch in the entrance passage: a homage to Wren in which the inner moulding is detached and held in place by voussoir stones. This is a personal Mannerist device – a sort of deconstruction of Classical forms – which Lutyens played with again and again, as in his late war-memorial designs like the Australian Memorial at Villers-Bretonneaux.

Lutyens wrote again from the train back from Cromer in September 1899. 'Hillingdon's very kind and Lord H. gives me all I want. Lady H. wants to rebuild Overstrand Church and I hope she may!' – she didn't, although Lutyens did get to design the strange little Methodist church in Overstrand for Lord Battersea – '… Lady Hillingdon is a funny person. She said at lunch – talking about when the house would be finished – "at all events if the house is not finished we shall have you". This was greeted with a roar of laughter – and she tried to explain it away but couldn't, and then said "to explain the plans". What do you think she meant? Her remarks are always inane and helpless – always kind. She seems to live in a dream – sat upon – but never loses her even temper, nor does she seem to mind it very much. I like Lord H. awfully. Although he bullies her I don't think he means it unkindly and her apathy is rather riling. He is clever – quite, most amusing, a pleasant modest and keen insight into matters of art and men, practical, economical and not unduly mean …'.[103]

Overstrand Hall was first photographed by *Country Life* for Lawrence Weaver's book, published in 1913.

The south and east fronts: each symmetrical with projecting oriel end bays; each equipped with open loggias – two on the east front – and each very strange in character.

SEVEN

DEANERY GARDEN

Deanery Garden may be regarded as the quintessential Lutyens house: a semi-rural retreat which is a dream of old England, superbly built of the most sympathetic materials, and yet a pure formal conception of the utmost brilliance in which house and garden are integrated. And as the house was designed for Edward Hudson, the creator of *Country Life*, it represented the ideal of the magazine by presenting an image which was promoted in its pages. As far as Christopher Hussey was concerned, 'Deanery Garden, Sonning, may be called without overstatement a perfect architectural sonnet, compounded of brick and tile and timber forms, in which his handling of the masses and spaces serve as a rhythm: its theme, a romantic bachelor's idyllic afternoons beside a Thames backwater.' 'Sonning is coming on all right I think,' wrote Lutyens to his wife in September 1901. The Deanery Garden had been conceived in 1899 and it was the first of Lutyens's designs for 'Huddy', who published the unnamed result in his magazine four years later, on 9 May 1903, under the title 'A House and a Garden'.

'We can imagine a poet some four or five years ago standing in the quiet lane and looking at the rustic village, building here his dream house, with ancient boundary walls whereon herbs and flowers grew, fragrant and old fashioned, here a mass of ivy hiding the brickwork, and there a spray of roses blushing above it ...'. And, continued the anonymous author, 'The poet's dream came true. So naturally has the house been planned that it seems to have grown out of the landscape rather than to have been fitted into it. No conceivable modern building could harmonise more perfectly with the village, the old church that stands opposite, and the woodlands rising far away on the edge of the horizon.' Yet the house is also a structured architectural conception of great brilliance.

Hudson had bought an old orchard in the centre of Sonning, a secret garden behind an old brick wall, to build his house in. The entrance is modest: a simple arched opening in this wall. But this front door instantly announces the formal geometry that governs the design and links it to the formal garden beyond which Lutyens designed with Gertrude Jekyll. A passage vaulted in brick and clunch, or hard chalk, forms a straight axis which leads directly to another door, past a courtyard to the right and a glimpse of garden through an arch to the left. This straight line then continues through the house, past the timber staircase on one side and then, as in a 'screens passage', through the double-height, half-timbered hall infilled with clunch and with its giant timber oriel, then out into the garden, over a 'bridge terrace', with a pool and a long rill stretching away on one side, and then down curved, concentric steps to the less formal garden beyond. A second unifying axis works at right angles to the entrance passageway, from the open tank court through another vaulted passage and out towards a pergola.

The principal garden elevation is a masterly composition of a few basic elements, with the horizontality of the mellow, red-brick wall broken only by the huge timber oriel with its forty-eight lights of small leaded panes, and, on the other side of the garden door, by the great chimney-breast with its triple stack shooting up towards the sky, whose chamfered flank runs flush into the angled side of the door – a piece of subtle simplicity, a treatment of ravishing directness of a sort that is found throughout the house.

But Lutyens did not let cleverness for its own sake overtake his sense of what a house should be. Although the house is full of incident and subtlety within a small space, it is the domesticity,

the earthiness, the sheer romantic Englishness of Deanery Garden that made it a dream house. This quality is enhanced by Lutyens's assured handling of the roofs. On the garden front he achieved dignity by the great unbroken length of tiles above the high walls, expressing the pitch as gables only on the shorter side elevations, while on the street side two great planes of roof come right down low, almost touching the old boundary wall.

The interior of Deanery Garden was planned around the double-height hall which, as the photographs taken by Charles Latham reveal, was simply furnished by Hudson with antique English oak furniture, Turkey carpets and old pewter. 'This bold conception of the Hall takes its place so happily as the climax of the design,' wrote A. S. G. Butler much later, 'that we overlook the restlessness of those great oak pieces entwining themselves between the chalk blocking of the walls.'[104] The upper floor is reached by a staircase that is a masterpiece of traditional craftsmanship, with every piece properly tenoned and pegged in place. This leads to the upper corridor, built of solid oak timbers and partly cantilevered out into the central court, 'sufficient to make a long and quite habitable room' complete with its own fireplace.

As for the garden, that masterpiece of formal geometry in brick, stone and tile, earth, grass and water, 'it is to the low terraced walls that we look for the glorious effects which are to be produced by the bold use of those plants which love to thrust their roots into the crannies or crevices of brick and stonework'.[105] Such were the effects intended by Gertrude Jekyll, who had brought Lutyens and Hudson together, while it was her young architect who planned the long thin canal in the water garden which runs parallel to the house from the bridge terrace to a round tank to the west, and the pergola at right angles to that axis which encloses the garden in front of the east elevation of brick, tile and timber. Weaver noted that 'Miss Jekyll worked with the architect in producing effects of singular

Preceding pages (left): *The south-east front of Deanery Garden, seen from the pergola that connects the gardens with a door in the old boundary wall.*
(right): *The magnificent south-west front, seen from the orchard below the terrace and formal garden: the convex and concave curved steps are typical of Lutyens.*

Above: *The tank court, looking across the vaulted entrance passage towards the gardens to the south-east: the pergola can be seen in the distance.*

Right: *The hall, with its huge oriel window, seen from the screens passage. The door in the panelling to the right leads to the dining room.*

richness. It may well be that it was the fine old enclosing wall of the Deanery Garden, with its massive buttresses and well-wrought coping, which has since encouraged Mr Lutyens to be generous with materials in the building of garden walls.' And even A. S. G. Butler was impressed, writing in 1950 of 'an instance of the utmost fusion by architecture of a house and garden. Each enhances the other and neither, by itself, is complete.'[106]

'Mr Lutyens never designed a more perfect house or a more charming garden,' concluded *Country Life* in 1903 – the year Hudson sold it. Charles Latham took the photographs for that article and he included Deanery Garden in the first volume of *In English Homes* the following year. As first built, the house was almost square in plan around three sides of the courtyard, but Lutyens later enlarged it before 1912 for C. W. Christie-Miller by adding a new north-west wing in the same soft red brick, but in a more suave, streamlined-Tudor style. And in July 1927, Lutyens wrote to his wife that 'Sonning is being added to again' (it has been spoiled since).

Two years after that, the young Henry-Russell Hitchcock delivered the praise of the house in his early book on modern architecture, earlier quoted [page 24], and he continued that

Left: *The staircase of oak with masonry walls of clunch, which was also used to infill the spaces between the massive timbers.*

Top: *The wide first-floor corridor, which is cantilevered out over the Fountain Court – a room in itself complete with a fireplace.*

Above: *The dining room, with an old oak table and the sideboard loaded with Hudson's collection of china and pewter.*

'The quality of the plain brickwork and the plain oak beams at the great bay-window, the fine balance of the irregular masses, the skill displayed in the entrance arch of many brick orders, an architectural feature suggestive but not imitative of the past, the perfect adaptation of the plan to contemporary life, have hardly been equalled.'[107]

Indeed, Deanery Garden has always been perhaps the most consistently admired of Lutyens's houses. Pevsner, in 1951, enjoyed the 'contrast and surprise' in the geometry of the famous south front, while, two years earlier, John Betjeman and John Piper described it as 'a brick house of genius ... [which] in its picturesque solidity and its feeling of comfort in rich simplicity was a revolutionary essay which had influence'.[108] Yet 'Huddy' only spent weekends in his dream house for a couple of years before selling it on.

Left: *The house and garden seen from the pergola above the circular pool at the north-west end of the narrow canal.*

Above: *The half-timber and red-brick gable above the sitting room on the south-east elevation.*

EIGHT

GREY WALLS

Grey Walls – originally called High Walls – is one of two houses that Lutyens built in Scotland. Both are unusual. But whereas
The Ferry Inn at Rosneath in the west shows the architect experimenting with the Art Nouveau, Grey Walls in the east at Gullane is an
essay in geometry that unites the Classical and the vernacular. Lutyens once described this house as his favourite,
yet it was only a summer holiday home.

The 'patron' was the Hon. Alfred Lyttelton, a Unionist MP, and the youngest child of the 4th Lord Lyttelton of Hagley.
Lyttelton seems to have been almost too good to be true: a sportsman and cricketer, involved with the Souls, he knew all the right people
and became a great help to Lutyens – getting him the job of designing the churches in the centre of Hampstead Garden Suburb.

His second wife was Edith Balfour, known as 'DD', who was related to Lady Emily Lutyens by marriage, and Lyttelton served as
Colonial Secretary in Arthur Balfour's Cabinet. A compulsive golfer, Lyttelton bought land next to the Muirfield Links overlooking the
Firth of Forth, the home of the Honourable Company of Edinburgh Golfers.

In April 1899, Lady Emily told her husband that her sister 'says the DD Lytteltons are bent on building a house – that they have made an offer for a piece of land in Scotland … . DD told her they wanted to employ you … . Alfred has seen your work in Surrey and greatly admires it and raves of Bumps's house. DD said there were points she would insist on – as for instance she would have big windows, plenty that opened and that she could get out of. She could not bear a dark room and she thought your little windows did not give enough light. So if you get the job you will have to remember this … . Their approval might be a very good thing for you and their blame do you a good deal of harm, and your reputation is rather that of being extravagant and not exact about money …'[109]

Lutyens did as he was told. The interiors are light and Classical. And he looked at local buildings and made High Walls of rubble stone, with roofs of grey Dutch pantiles which were also used to enhance window lintels. The plan of the house is odd; it is as if a small symmetrical H-plan house with wings has been rammed into another building with a concave front, but all is explained by the peculiarities of the site. The links are to the north and the approach

Preceding pages (left): The corridor sitting room leading from the entrance of Grey Walls to the drawing room in the north-east wing.
(right): The concave entrance front seen from the gate piers at the southern end of the diagonal approach to the house.

Above: The main entrance: a Mannerist Classical composition with console brackets and a broken pediment framing a pedestal.

Right: The concave entrance with the western flanking chimney-breast: note the subtle recessions in the wall above the first-floor windows.

Above: *Two of the three lodges added in 1909 at the end of the drive;
behind the left-hand lodge a garage is carefully concealed.*

Below: *The view through the west window of the open-air tea-room
next to the dining room.*

The more informal south-east front looking on to the formal gardens; the tea-room is on the right.

is from the south, while the formal garden was placed in front of the principal rooms and separated from the long forecourt by one of the several sinuous high walls, topped with pantiles, that grow out of the house and divide up the grounds.

The symmetrical concave entrance front – or screen – is extra-ordinary, with a Baroque doorcase in the centre and the long curving walls terminated by bold chimney-breasts at either side. This curve reconciles two geometries on plan, for the main part of the house and the service wing were designed on a right-angled grid, but the approach from the coast road comes in at an angle of 45 degrees. This precise formality was reinforced when, in 1909, three lodges or 'bothies' were built by the entrance. The arriving visitor now faces the central one, whose door has a mannered Gibbs surround above which a hipped cottage roof rises. On either side are pairs of gate piers, each at an angle of 45 degrees, so connecting with the existing diagonal geometry and presenting the visitor with a choice of direction – such was Lutyens's love of ambiguity.

At the beginning of 1902, Lutyens wrote from nearby Gosford (Lord Wemyss's monster seat by Adam, enlarged by William

Young with 'so many technical mistakes') that Grey Walls was 'getting on slowly. The Lytteltons love the grey tiles – ain't that comforting? Lady Wemyss likes it too.'[110] The Lytteltons first used High Walls the following August. Four more happy golfing summers followed before they decided that they could not afford the luxury. The house was then bought by William James, that rich friend of King Edward VII, who built the lodges. It was Mrs James who had already commissioned Lutyens to design Monkton on their West Dean estate, and it was her son, the Surrealist and collector, Edward James, born at Grey Walls in 1907, who trans-formed that Sussex 'trianon' into a unique fantasy.

Grey Walls was described by Lawrence Weaver and illustrated in *Country Life* on 9 September 1911 with photographs by Francis Caird Inglis. Golf continues today at Muirfield and the house now functions as a hotel and restaurant, making it one of the few masterpieces by Lutyens which can readily be enjoyed by visitors.

NINE

HOMEWOOD

Homewood at Knebworth is a comparatively small house which Lutyens designed for his mother-in-law. Hussey was a little dismissive, describing it as 'in essence one of those pretty little gabled houses, with weather-tiled upper floors, to which the young aspire and the elderly withdraw, but which Lutyens here converted into a rustic trianon'. But it is more than that; Homewood is a brilliant, compact essay in planning and a highly sophisticated design in which vernacular forms are combined with Classical formality. Lutyens had married the daughter of an Earl: the 1st Lord Lytton, Viceroy of India, who had died in 1891. His widow, the Dowager Countess, who had at first opposed her daughter's marriage to an architect (not quite a gentleman, hence the contemporary debate over whether architecture was a profession or a trade), soon became very close to her son-in-law. Homewood was designed as a dower house for her on the Knebworth Estate and it was paid for by her son Victor, the 2nd Earl.

In fact, it was intended both for his mother and for her unmarried daughter, Constance. Lutyens corresponded with both his mother- and sister-in-law about the evolving design of their house in 1900 and it was built the following year.

Later, under the influence of her sister Emily, Lady Constance became a determined and courageous suffragette – she was imprisoned four times for her actions and her health was ruined by forced feeding in jail by the authorities. 'Constance Lytton,' wrote Roger Fulford, 'illumines the rather wild years of militancy with the radiant colours of courage and devotion, made the more conspicuous because they emerge from a background of meekness and simplicity.'[111] It was Arthur Chapman, of Crooksbury, who in 1910 discovered that she was held in Walton Gaol under a false name and helped Emily (who never condoned violence) to bring her home. It is a mistake to think of the Edwardian years as a golden Indian summer, for it was a time of tension and deep social unrest both in and outside Parliament. And this impinged on Lutyens. There was not only the militancy of his sister-in-law, but through Emily he also encountered Emmeline and F. W. Pethick-Lawrence, who edited *Votes for Women*, were imprisoned for demonstrating in favour of women's suffrage – and had bought a Lutyens house in Surrey, Mascot at South Holmwood, to which he added a billiard room.

Homewood is full of surprises. The entrance front is approached axially, although this vista is at first concealed from the drive. Three of the four elevations are symmetrical and each is different. And the two principal elevations – front and back – combine rustic vernacular motifs with sophisticated Classical games. On the entrance front, below three weather-boarded gables, are short rusticated pilasters with, in the centre, a remarkable Mannerist doorcase in which a flat arch runs across the segmental pediment, leaving a void above. And facing the gardens and terrace a five-bay façade articulated with a double-height Ionic order of pilasters is embraced and overwhelmed by sweeping planes of tiled roof. It is as if a Classical villa has been adapted as a farm-house.

'People sometimes talk as though architecture had come to an end, as though there is nothing to be done except to copy the work of our forefathers,' remarked Lawrence Weaver. 'This garden front of Homewood is a small, albeit delightful thing in itself, but it is symptomatic of much. It proves, what people are slow to believe, that in the new arrangement of traditional forms, perhaps themselves of widely differing provenance, there is room for infinite originality. We do not want new forms, but new light on the old,

Preceding pages (left): *The twin-gabled, weather-boarded side elevation of Homewood, the house Lutyens designed for his mother-in-law.*
(right): *The north-west-facing entrance front with its ground-floor rusticated order and the Mannerist doorcase placed centrally below three weather-boarded, rustic gables.*

Left: *The garden front with a terrace and twin open loggias facing south-east, all contained within the sweep of tiled roof that embraces the double-height Ionic order.*

a new perception of their possibilities …'. But for Peter Inskip, 'While it might be appropriate for the home of a dowager countess to be concerned with romantic decay, the intended enlargement eventually seems to inflate the house to an overblown scale and the hermetic world of idiosyncratic jokes becomes possibly precious and even overblown in its monotony.'[112]

Surprises continue inside. Although Homewood seems at first like a compact square on plan, the garden front is, in fact, not on the same axis as the entrance. The Mannerist entrance does not contain a door but announces a vaulted passage off which the front door opens on one side. This leads to a vestibule, which leads to a hall, from which the staircase rises across the plan. 'What gave the house a sense of spaciousness,' recalled Mary Lutyens, 'was the very wide main staircase with shallow treads leading up from the inner hall and lit by the glass roof of the first-floor landing. The stairs were carpeted in apple green with wide verges of glossy white paint… . There was no electricity and I associate it with the cosy smell of oil lamps which left black smudges on the ceilings. Our grandmother never used the bathroom. Throughout her long life – she died in 1936 at the age of ninety-five – she preferred a tin tub in front of her bedroom fire.'[113]

There seem to have been some problems with the completed house. 'It makes me miserable to think that you are not absolutely happy, absolutely content, absolutely comfortable in a house of mine!' Lutyens wrote to his wife in 1904. 'You of all dear people. Homewood is much better than Crooksbury I think as regards architecture etc., and when it all grows up and the sore places in the grounds heal up, it will look very well, but what do this matter if you are cold and draught ridden?'[114] The *Country Life* photographs seem to have been taken for Weaver's book and tend – deliberately? – to exaggerate the size of this little masterpiece.

Right: *The top-lit first-floor landing and gallery above the staircase. The use of half-height white-painted Tuscan columns was typical of Lutyens.*

Below: *The staircase climbing up from the hall; the door on the left leads to the entrance vestibule, that on the right to the dining room.*

TEN

MARSH COURT

Marsh Court was the last and largest of Lutyens's essays in his free 'Tudor' style, but – unlike so many contemporary houses that revelled in Englishness and tradition – it could never be mistaken for an old house. Lutyens's handling of the style is suave and controlled, while the house is also unusual in terms of his use of materials. Marsh Court is white – originally brilliant white – because it is built of hard chalk, or clunch. Inside and out, the house demonstrates Lutyens's happy mastery of traditional building materials.

Designed in 1901, Marsh Court was built on a spur overlooking the River Test in Hampshire, and Lutyens would fish there when he went to stay with the client, Herbert Johnson, '"adventurer", stockjobber, and sportsman', who had seen and admired his work in the pages of *Country Life*. He had already made half a million in the City; he later lost a fortune and made another.

Hussey considered him 'the ideal type of Lutyens client', but he was more: '"Johnnie" and Ned, perceiving one another's greatnesses, became life-long friends. Lutyens came to love his courage, vigour and honesty which, with more than a touch of flamboyance, he worked into the building.' Clunch had been used inside churches and for cottages, but never as the principal building material for a house on this scale. Here, the whiteness of the walls was enhanced by contrast with the tall red-brick chimneys and the long, unbroken sweeps of pitched tile roof.

The texture of the walls was also emphasised by the introduction of small squares of knapped flint, or patches of red tile, as if they had long ago been patched, or perhaps raised on the site of an older building. This is certainly analogous to the fake, built-in history in earlier houses by, say, George Devey. But Lutyens's introduction of 'archaeology' could not possibly be mistaken for the real thing; rather, it is Mannerism in materials, playing with the idea of the past. This is evident where the squares of flint are regularly spaced in a pattern, as on the pier of the arched loggia.

The house is both formal and informal. The north entrance court is precisely symmetrical, but on the garden elevation the projecting south-west wing is balanced not by another but by a sunken pool, an elaborate composition of steps, balustrades and piers – Goodhart-Rendel observed with a certain justice that 'at Marsh Court is one of those complicated gardens full of architecture and water which photograph very well but do not perhaps add very greatly to the pleasure of life'.[115]

The entrance arch is one of Lutyens's essays in Mannerism, or deconstructed Classicism, with the inner stone arch moulding made

Preceding pages (left): The garden front of Marsh Court seen from the west – the sunken pool garden is behind the balustrade.
(right): The north-facing entrance front with the concave steps leading to the lower gardens in the foreground.

Above: The staircase of oak with the solid walls between the massive timbers infilled with clunch.

Right: The pool garden stretching south from the west wing, with the distant Hampshire countryside visible above the containing balustrade.

separate from the tunnel vault and held in place by three voussoir stones. Inside the house, although there are half-timbered staircases and corridors, the principal rooms are firmly Classical. The hall, with its rich, heavy plaster ceiling has a screen of Palladian design with Doric columns. The best, perhaps, is the billiard room, with its table resting on a colossal, carefully moulded piece of clunch – so providing chalk for the players' cues. Writing in *Country Life*, L. March Phillips was concerned to emphasise the 'thoroughly English character' of Lutyens's work, praising the 'massiveness of treatment' which he thought contrasted with 'Renaissance ostentation'. Marsh Court was one of the few early houses to be published elsewhere. In *The Studio* (the art journal which promoted Voysey, Baillie-Scott and Mackintosh) in 1909, G. Lloyd Morris thought the house exhibited that 'unity' which 'is the pre-eminent quality underlying the orderly and tranquil beauty manifest in Mr Lutyens's houses. He never fails in this respect; one may cavil at certain details, or question the use and treatment of a material, but in the handling of the general conception there is always a breadth and a certainty in the composition that remain in the memory long after the details may have been forgotten.'[116]

Marsh Court was finished in 1904, but Johnson altered and

Left: *Inside the twin-arched loggia in the south-east wing: note the regular pattern of knapped-flint panels climbing up the circular pier.*

Below (left): *Inside the entrance porch, looking north through Lutyens's deconstructed arch.*
(right): *What was originally the principal bathroom over the front porch.*

improved it over the years and installed more bathrooms. In 1924–26, Lutyens added a Great Hall, or ballroom, to the south-west and, unusually, continued the same language while refining and simplifying it. He last visited the house on a tour he made in 1940 with Christopher Hussey when 'he resolved he could not pass so near to Marsh Court without looking up Herbert Johnson. There we were pressed to stay the night, and Lutyens listened to the organ played in the ballroom that was the latest addition to his *tour-de-force* in chalk building … and talked far into the night with our host.'

Marsh Court was illustrated in *Country Life* for 1 September 1906 and Charles Latham used his photographs again in the second volume of his *In English Homes*. The house was covered again by Lawrence Weaver on 19 April 1913, and the later additions were photographed for Christopher Hussey's articles published on 19 and 26 March 1932. At the conclusion of his 1906 article L. March Phillips wrote that 'It looks a genuine bit of England, and as I left it I could easily imagine its walls hallowed already by associations of romance and sentiment such as cling to old English homes'. 'But,' wrote Hussey, 'revisiting Marsh Court after thirty years, one is more conscious of its forecasting of contemporary standards than of its summarising of the immediate past.' Houses by Lutyens present a wide and sometimes paradoxical range of images, allowing very different interpretations. At once modern and traditional, formal and Picturesque, Classical and romantic: there is something in them for everybody.

ELEVEN

LITTLE THAKEHAM

For Lutyens, Little Thakeham in Sussex was the house that he once described as 'the best of the bunch'. It at first may look like a nostalgic *Country Life* dream: an old, mellow Elizabethan manor house on the edge of the South Downs. But it is not quite what it seems.

This house, for Christopher Hussey, was clear evidence 'that Lutyens's accomplishment had by now attained the pitch at which the loose articulations of his romantic work hitherto were becoming too easy to stimulate his imagination. He needed to get his teeth into the more complex, more resistant medium of the Orders. Looking at the elevations of Thakeham again in this light, at the beautiful clarity of the garden plan, one realises that it is essentially classical in all but style.' So, behind the symmetrical gabled front with the giant oriel there is a double-height Baroque hall.

The story of Little Thakeham is complicated, and mildly scandalous, as Jane Brown describes in her book on *Lutyens and the Edwardians*. The client was Ernest Murray Blackburn, known as 'Tom', whose father had done well in New York importing Madeira before returning home to Devon. Tom Blackburn had been to Winchester and Oxford and survived as a schoolmaster until 1887 when he inherited £80,000. He then became a country gentleman and gardener. In 1901, he bought 26 acres near Storrington and commissioned a house from J. Hatchard Smith, a dim London architect. Blackburn eventually found he did not care for the brick building that was rising: it was 'a large blot on the beautiful landscape …

fit for Wimbledon or Putney, rather than a country house', and on 29 April 1902 he recorded in his diary that 'I disagree with Mr Hatchard Smith, and Mr E. L. Lutyens came down to the site, and advised that the house should be pulled down, and that a house of Pulborough rock should be built on one side of it, keeping the old kitchen and scullery. The house was already built nearly up to the first floor and all the window frames were made. Messrs Norman and Burt agree to take back all the doors which had been made, and to try and sell the window frames.'[117]

The result was a new job. Hatchard Smith was paid off (with £550, or 4½ per cent), but when he found that his creation was being pulled down, he wrote a furious letter to the *Building News*, whose editor published his original half-timbered and red-brick design for 'Thakeham Court' and announced in an editorial that, when a client changed his mind, any 'second' architect should decline to give advice. So, in the ensuing correspondence, Blackburn retorted that 'here seems to be a view entertained by many architects and most building papers that houses are built in order to display the skill and taste of the architect. This is not the case. Houses are built for men to live in, and those who live in them are entitled to have them built to suit their fancy and con-

venience.' And Lutyens was subsequently exonerated from Hatchard Smith's charge of professional misconduct by the Royal Institute of British Architects.

Oswald P. Milne, the future architect of Claridge's, later recalled that after Lutyens had first visited Blackburn, 'when he got back to London that evening he handed me two sheets of squared paper with the house completely worked out in sketch form with all the plans, sections and elevations. He must have done the whole thing on the train. He asked me to get to work at once on the scale drawings. Little Thakeham as built is almost exactly to the sketch which he made in that way.'[118] But Margaret Richardson has pointed out that other surviving drawings reveal that the final solution was not reached quite so quickly or easily. She also notes

Preceding pages (left): *Tudor and Baroque: the oriel bay window to the hall on the south front of Little Thakeham.*
(right): *The north entrance front, seen from the road that runs right in front of the house. The service court is to the left.*

Right: *The hall looking west; the staircase is behind the screen and the balcony on the right leads off the first-floor corridor.*

Below: *The south-facing garden front; this elevation is symmetrical either side of the central oriel window.*

that the design may well have been inspired by Mapledurham House, which Lutyens had visited in 1898.

At Little Thakeham, vernacular Tudor and the Grand Manner are combined. A large double-height space running the whole length of the garden elevation between the wings is divided by a hall screen which abuts the arch of the central projecting oriel bay. This stone screen is pierced by two doorways with Gibbs surrounds, behind which a staircase rises to balconies on two levels above the screen, overlooking the hall. Here are intimate spaces within a larger space, providing an almost child-like sense of mystery and romance – typical of Lutyens. Nicholas Taylor has observed that all this is 'exterior' architecture – indeed, similar balconies appear *outside* Heathcote.

The other glory of Little Thakeham is the garden, with the terraces and various gardens at different levels and the long pergola

Left: *The bedrooms in the west wing: note the quality of the rustic country doors, with hinges, latches and locks all designed by the architect.*

Above: *The first-floor corridor, looking west – the main staircase is to the left just before the steps that lead to the principal bedrooms.*

axial with the central oriel – all carefully planted by Blackburn. 'I got to Thakeham about eight,' Lutyens reported in July 1904. 'A most divine evening. The great downs bathed in reflected light and the garden wonderfully good. Blackburn is very slow, apparently, but is really an artist and he does little at a time but what he does is singularly good I think. He has made the pergola delightful – in a way quite his own – with hollyhocks – and to enjoy the effect he postpones planting the more permanent things. His attitude is so unlike the general of people – like leaving a picture unfinished to enjoy the initial stages. The children's gardens are very amusing … . The lawn is covered with guinea pigs …'[119]

Blackburn and his family had moved in five months earlier. He was £20,000 overdrawn and the house had cost him £10,500 – £13,000 including the stables and gardens – when Hatchard Smith's design (with stables) had been estimated at a total of £8,400, but he was pleased with his architect and his creation. Little Thakeham was published in *Country Life* for 28 August 1909. Since 1979 it has been open to the public as a hotel and restaurant.

TWELVE

LINDISFARNE CASTLE

Lindisfarne was Lutyens's first castle and his second house for Edward Hudson. In January 1902, Lutyens reported from Grey Walls: 'Just got a telewire from Hudson saying he has got Lindisfarne Castle – will I go and look at it as I am up here so I had better. It will be amusing.'[120] St Aidan had established a church on Lindisfarne, or Holy Island, off the Northumberland coast and later a monastery was built there by the Bishop of Durham. The tall rock at the end of the island had been fortified by the English Crown in 1570–72 as a base for forays into Scotland. Oddly enough, the derelict and uninhabitable fort that Hudson acquired had been sketched only six months before by Charles Rennie Mackintosh. His drawings emphasise the sublime monumentality of the faceted planes of tough stone wall rising from the rock, and these were the elements that inspired Lutyens in his restoration.

Lutyens's designs for conversion were approved shortly after the Coronation of Edward VII in August 1902 at a party at Deanery Garden (which Hudson then sold). Lindisfarne was intended to be used as a holiday home and Lutyens had to make it habitable and create bedrooms (and a single bathroom). He hardly altered the rugged silhouette of the abandoned Tudor castle and the new work was done in the same materials and in the simple spirit of the old. The result is highly romantic and the route to and through the building is both external and internal, rising up ramps and stairs to reach a succession of terraces, with new shapes and new spaces constantly emerging.

Inside, the spaces are low and simple. Much of the fabric is original, as with the stone vault of the Ship Room. In the entrance hall Lutyens added massive round columns, reminiscent of the Norman work at Durham Cathedral. But they are not 'neo-Norman' (most horrid of styles) as the arches above fade into them while the fat shafts themselves have no bases where they rise from the stone floor. As Hussey wrote, 'The poetry of the building derives from the effects having been got almost entirely by structural means – walls, vaults, apertures – and in the avoiding of all but the broadest suggestion of "period". Consequently there is no hint of faking and so of make belief: the new masonry is as generously devised as the old but its profiles are not copies, they are solutions attained by reviewing the old mason's traditions afresh: the romance is real.'

The austerity of the interiors at Lindisfarne was as deliberate as the abstraction and simplicity of the architectural forms. As Peter Inskip has written, 'The "spartan life" intended for the Barings at Lambay and Hudson at Lindisfarne was supported by whitewashed walls and oak floors painted duck-egg blue or crimson with a thin coat of white paint dragged over. The furniture was seventeenth-century oak, mainly stripped of all polish and bleached, and simple eighteenth-century rush-seated ladder-back chairs supplemented with the occasional piece in the same manner designed by the architect.'[121] The restoration work was completed by 1906, although the north bedrooms off Lutyens's Long Gallery were only added in 1912. Lindisfarne Castle was described by Peter Anderson Graham in *Country Life* for 7 June 1913.

Hudson would dispense lobsters and champagne to his guests. In May 1906, Lutyens went to stay there with Gertrude Jekyll, also accompanied by, for some reason, a raven. 'We arrived safely,' he reported to Lady Emily. 'Bumps not too tired. We have been moving furniture and I am very disinclined to write somehow.

Preceding pages (left): *The entrance hall created by Lutyens inside Lindisfarne Castle, with rugged new columns and arches fitted within the old fabric.* (right): *The entrance front seen across the Lower Battery to the east; the door leads down to the approach ramp, and in the distance, across the water, is the Northumberland coast.*

Left: *The castle seen from the east with the approach ramp (Lutyens removed the parapet wall) leading up to the Lower Battery.*

The curtains are not ready yet which is a disappointment but I dare not show it as they have worked so hard and well. The raven was an awful anxiety on the journey and carrying her on my lap across the sands … . Bumps is quite charmed and so appreciative and we all had good nights.' Later, in 1911, Miss Jekyll laid out a small walled garden near the Castle.

Even more anxious-making were the Royal visitors who came to inspect the castle two years later: the future King George V and Queen Mary. 'The Prince was awfully bored apparently with the lecture given by some archaeologist and looked at his watch every two minutes … . [Arthur] Bigge was walking with the Prince and I heard him say, you know Sir this place has been rebuilt by E. Lutyens. So I hollered out High Stop, I'm here. The Prince nearly had a fit of laughter. He said, how verry goode, ha ha and told everybody. When I told him how I had proposed to drain the Castle with a gun etc. he said "oh yes, drains, of course drains" without a smile. He was terribly alarmed at the gangway up and wanted a wall built. I told him we had pulled one down and that if he really thought it unsafe we would put nets out. He thought that very funny. The Princess couldn't bear the cobbles, they hurt her

feet. I told her we were very proud of them! The only thing she specially admired were some fleur-de-lis on a fireback. Hudson said he was dreadfully nervous and I think they made each other stiff. The Prince was awfully anxious to get away when he found the tide was rising, for a sailor I thought him over nervous.'[122]

Easier summer guests included the cellist Guilhermina Suggia, the ballerina Alicia Markova, the conductor Malcolm Sargent, and such writers as Elizabeth von Arnim and Lytton Strachey. The Lutyens family often came to stay, although Lady Emily found the castle cold and uncomfortable. Hudson sold Lindisfarne Castle in 1921, and in 1944 it was given to the National Trust by Sir Edward de Stein and so is open to the public.

Above: *Looking west past the massive new pier introduced by Lutyens towards the new Long Gallery leading to the Upper Battery.*

Right: *Barbara Lutyens, known as 'Barbie' – the architect's first and favourite child – photographed by Charles Latham in the Long Gallery in 1910: one of a series of studies commissioned by Edward Hudson.*

THIRTEEN

PAPILLON HALL

Papillon Hall, near Market Harborough in Leicestershire, was one of Lutyens's strangest and most mysterious houses, whose intriguing design can now only be appreciated from the *Country Life* photographs taken for Lawrence Weaver's 1913 book because it is the only significant work by the architect to have been destroyed.

The core of Papillon Hall was a semi-fortified, stone octagonal house built in 1622–24 by David Papillon, master jeweller and military engineer, who advised King Charles I on the sale of jewellery. In 1903, it was bought by Captain Frank Ashton Bellville, heir to a fortune in Keen's mustard, 'who did little else but hunt'. Mrs Bellville, who had met Lutyens at a party at Deanery Garden, asked him to enlarge this curious house. Lutyens responded either to the unusual geometry of Papillon Hall or to its Huguenot name, for he proposed adding radiating wings off the diagonal sides of the flattened octagon to create a fashionable Edwardian 'butterfly' plan.

Such plans, designed to capture more of the sun during the day, had been used by Arts and Crafts architects like Blow, Prior and Schultz, but Lutyens's immediate inspiration may well have been Chesters, the Classical house by Norman Shaw, which he had seen in 1901 and found 'lovely and loveable in great and many respects, but there are mistakes which I could not help thinking I should have avoided … . Yet the planning of it all is a masterpiece …'.[123]

New radiating wings containing a dining room and a drawing room were added to the east, and to the west a billiard room. Between this last and the existing service wing, Lutyens created a circular open Basin Court connecting the new main entrance with the vestibule within the original octagon. This plan produced some interesting conjunctions of forms, with the single-storey circular court abutting the gabled polygony of the house behind. Lutyens also introduced 'motifs which seem to have nothing to do with each other,' as Nikolaus Pevsner put it. '[T]his playing-up of contrasts sometimes just to amuse, but sometimes also *pour épater le bourgeois*, is in my opinion one of the most characteristic features of Lutyens's style.'[124] Most of Papillon Hall was designed in a simple vernacular manner, with roughcast walls, and between the chimney-breasts on drawing and dining rooms facing east over the gardens, the central gable sported half-timbering. Yet in the Basin Court, an inner ring of Tuscan columns supported the circular balcony, while the new entrance below a pair of leaded-light windows is a powerful, pedimented composition with rusticated Doric columns. This use of block rustication together with an arch breaking through the entablature showed Lutyens's growing interest in the games played by Palladio, but it is also intriguingly reminiscent of the customs *barrières* around Paris designed by the 'revolutionary' architect C.-N. Ledoux (who was himself influenced by English Palladianism).

Having been occupied by the U.S. 82nd Airborne Division, Papillon Hall was put up for sale in 1948 and pulled down two years later. Although so many country houses were demolished owing to changed conditions after the Second World War, there seem to have been peculiar circumstances surrounding the abandonment of this house. When Frank Bellville purchased Papillon Hall, a tiny cupboard with a padlocked metal grille in the lintel of the internal window over the original hall fireplace contained a pair of early-eighteenth-century women's shoes of green brocade, and the title deeds stated that 'on no account to permit them to be removed from the house, or ill-fortune would assuredly befall the owner'.[125] During the enlargement of the house, these shoes were

Preceding pages (left): *The new entrance portico added to Papillon Hall, seen from the north-west through an arch in the concave wall screening the stables.*
(right): *The east front with its dash of domesticated half-timber; the drawing room was in the wing to the left, the dining room to the right.*

Right: *The drawing room with its coved plaster ceiling designed by Lutyens in the new wing projecting south-east from the original octagonal core of the old house.*

Left: *The circular Basin Court Lutyens placed between his new entrance and the old house; the lamp indicates the opening from the outer portico.*

Above: *The garden house and gate piers at the end of a vista from the house looking towards open countryside.*

taken to Bellville's solicitors for safe keeping. In April 1904, Lutyens recorded that Bellville was perturbed by the slow progress of the work: accidents had occurred, a workman had been killed, the local firm had abandoned the contract and an outside contractor had to be found. Furthermore, apparently, the skeleton of a woman was found walled up in the attics of the old house. This was believed to be the Spanish mistress of the second David Papillon, or 'Pamps', who had never been allowed to leave the house and who disappeared in suspicious circumstances in 1715. All this is recounted in a booklet by Colonel Pen Lloyd published in 1977 and entitled *The History of the Mysterious Papillon Hall*.

What is also certain is that, in August 1905, Lutyens wrote to his wife 'I am very distressed indeed to see in the papers that Frank Bellville has been upset out of his car and fractured his skull. His condition is critical *The Times* says. I do hope he will recover. I am really fond of him and like and admire so much of him. I do hope

nothing worse will happen and that he will recover and enjoy my Papps. It is odd the Papps prophecies and that this should happen. Everybody owning Papps is supposed to come to misfortune – the haunting red dog – the finding of a man and dog skeleton – the slipper legend – etc., etc. Do people recover from fractured skulls? Surely yes. He is so big and strong too and so really generous, patient and kind to his impossible wife ...'. He did recover, and in April 1908, Lutyens recorded that 'Frank Bellville looked in. His chauffeur and engineer has been killed in a motor smash and he wanted to know how to find another.'[126] This may, of course, merely confirm how dangerous was Edwardian motoring, but Colonel Pen Lloyd noted that, at the time, those shoes had been lent to an exhibition in Leicester. And he also recorded how, on two occasions during the war, American airmen who had removed the shoes did not return from missions over enemy territory.

Lutyens's daughter Ursula, Lady Ridley, visited Papillon Hall in 1950 just before it was demolished and wrote to Emily Lutyens that 'I feel rather relieved that it is going ... . His very worst Kingston By Pass manner in roughcast which is always ugly and a lot of half timber bogosity.'[127] But a fragment of the old house was rescued and installed in the gardens at Blagdon Hall.

FOURTEEN

FOLLY FARM

Folly Farm near Sulhamstead, Berkshire, was an early essay by Lutyens in what he called 'Wrennaissance' – that gentlemanly
Classical style in brick typical of the more formal houses of the late seventeenth and early eighteenth centuries. It was associated with the
domestic work of Sir Christopher Wren, whose addition to Hampton Court for King William III is a quintessential example of the style
and provided the inspiration for scores of Edwardian public libraries and town halls. But Folly Farm is not what it might seem,
for the Classical part of the house is the earlier part, while the wing in Lutyens's early and most romantic manner – an asymmetrical
composition of sweeping roofs, colossal chimneys and weather-boarded gables – was added later, when he was thinking of grand things like
New Delhi. Indeed, as Lawrence Weaver noted, this addition 'shows that the many houses which Lutyens has built …
in an austere Georgian manner, such as Great Maytham and The Salutation, have not lessened his skills in the use of earlier and more
traditional motifs … . It bears his personal impress in a very marked way, and every detail has been perfected so fully that even the
vegetable racks in the scullery are more interesting than the fittings of many a great library.'

The first phase of Folly Farm was built for H. H. Cochrane in 1905–06. Modest and neat, it is a symmetrical formal composition with projecting wings on an H-plan in the manner of William and Mary, built of the local Berkshire silver-grey bricks with red-brick trim next to the pre-existing farm. Here Lutyens played no games with the Orders: the composition relies on proportion and on the domestic character of the overall hipped roof. The games are all inside: the entrance placed centrally on the east-side elevation leads asymmetrically into the outer hall through a vestibule with two curved walls, while the double-height hall in the centre of the block is grandly Classical, with touches of Mannerism in the details (and walls originally painted black).

In 1912, Folly Farm was bought by Zachary Merton, mine-owner and philanthropist, whose new German wife, Antonie Rosalie Schmiechen, was a Theosophist who knew Lady Emily Lutyens and had known Madame Blavatsky. The Mertons needed more bedrooms and a larger dining room, so Lutyens provided these in a massive new wing. But he did not design this in the same style as the original house, as this would have overawed it and upset the symmetry. Instead, he opted for an extreme contrast and

designed what he called 'cowsheds' in his vernacular manner. A long corridor and the new dining room were placed at right angles around a water 'tank' and enclosed by an astonishing sweep of tiled roof, with a 'swept valley' at the corner, that comes down almost to the ground, just above the brick buttress arches containing a 'cloister'. The scale of this roof is enhanced by tiny dormers, and then there is another sweep of roof, this time long and horizontal above a two-storey, red-brick elevation which faces west across the garden, broken by a massive chimney-stack and a gabled balcony off the master bedroom.

In August 1913, Lutyens designed a fireback for the completed

Preceding pages (left): *The colossal chimney-breast and the balcony opening off the principal bedroom on the new west front added to Folly Farm in 1912.* (right): *The south front facing the formal gardens and the long canal; the 1906 house is on the right, the later 'cowshed' wing to the left.*

Below: *The new dining room in the 1912 wing, after being decorated by Lutyens's friend, the painter William Nicholson, in 1916.*

Right: *The double-height hall in the first, 1906, phase of the house: the walls were painted black, the woodwork and ceiling white and the balconies Venetian red.*

new wing, using the whole alphabet from A[ntonie] to Z[achary] with M[erton] in the middle, forming the date: MCMXII – 'It will look like a legend on a Huntley and Palmer biscuit, as made at Reading nearby'.[128] Christopher Hussey considered that, 'For sheer originality the Folly Farm twins are unique even in Lutyens's repertory'. And, as Roderick Gradidge has written, 'Well named, Folly Farm is in many ways Lutyens's most extravagant display of conspicuous consumption … . The long corridors and the enormous chimneys, and even the covered balcony, may have little functional justification, yet the resultant architecture is so splendid, and in a strange way so unpretentious, that we can forgive Lutyens his extravagances, particularly when we are not paying for them.'[129]

The Mertons certainly did, and Mrs Merton became a great friend to the Lutyens family, particularly after her husband's death in 1915. The following year she lent them Folly Farm for the summer holidays, 'complete with her excellent servants,' as Mary Lutyens recalled. '[I]t was to be the happiest summer of our family life … . It was a delicious house to live in with a great sense of space and luxury. William Nicholson was staying there painting murals for the dining-room so that the house was pervaded with my favourite smell of artist's studio … . In other parts of the house I remember yellow glossy paint. I believe there was a bedroom in which all the furniture, designed by Father, was painted primrose yellow … . Father gave all his houses a special feeling of his own. There was never anything in them to jar – rather, there was a sense of order, of harmony, that was both inspiring and restful.'[130]

Both phases of Folly Farm were photographed by F. Sleigh for Lawrence Weaver's book and then described by Christopher Hussey (with new photographs) in *Country Life* for 28 January and 4 February 1922 when the house was owned by Arthur Gilbey. After it changed hands again, a new owner added, 'without reference to father, a banal "covered" approach to the original house which merely robs it of homogeneity,' as Robert Lutyens complained. 'To this is further added a touch of irony in that the architect responsible – a woman – was at one time in my father's office. He may have had this fact in mind when replying to a journalist who asked for his opinion on the place of women in architecture. His reply was prompt. "As the wives of architects!" he answered.'[131] The offending architect was Clare Nauheim, but Lutyens's recorded attitude to women architects was probably a flippant aside, as he later employed Elisabeth Benjamin as an assistant. Folly Farm was altered again in 1965 by Francis Pollen for Hugh Astor.

The great 'cowshed' roof of the new wing, creating a cloister or loggia outside the new dining room: the 'swept valley' is between the two tiny dormer windows.

FIFTEEN

HEATHCOTE

'To those who know the triumphs that Mr E. L. Lutyens has won in the domain of traditional English architecture, the pictures of Heathcote will come with a shock of surprise, that cannot fail, however, to turn swiftly to pleasure,' announced Lawrence Weaver in *Country Life* for 9 July 1910. Many have been shocked by Heathcote since, for it is the house which has often been singled out as marking Lutyens's adoption of the Grand Manner, and so of the abandonment of the apparently forward-looking freedom of his earlier romantic houses. Yet Heathcote is a one-off. Never again – in a house – would he play such elaborate games with the Classical language. Ilkley was an unlikely place for Lutyens to have played his first serious game on Renaissance themes set by Palladio and Sanmicheli. The necessarily rich client, John Thomas Hemingway, had made a fortune with the Bradford wool exporters George Richardson & Co., and with his wife, a former mill-girl, had moved to a villa in Ilkley with a view towards Ilkley Moor. He had sent his children to be educated on the Continent and now wanted to build a smart new house.

On 4 May 1906, Lutyens recorded that he had received 'the awful Hemingway estimates, £17,000 odd the lowest!'[132] The final price was £17,500. Lutyens's attitude to his client is suggested by the story, already recounted [page 18], of the marble staircase that he installed contrary to Hemingway's wishes. In August 1906 he wrote to Emily that 'Hemingway asked about "Mrs Lutyens" – would you like to go up there? You would have fits – a coursed breakfast in slippers, boots put on in the sitting room sometimes used as a dining room and furnished as such – *en suite* but not so expensive as the real dining room. The ornaments – oh lor! And the walls of lincrusta with painted dado and frieze of flying sparrows, ferns and polyanthi displayed. And then a mass of modern prints from Academy pictures and electric lights galore …'[133]

Preceding pages (left): *The hall at Heathcote with its two Palladian screens of Doric columns made of green Siberian marble and one of Lutyens's favourite star light fittings.*
(right): *The garden front of Lutyens's exotic villa seen from the south from the lawn below the raised terrace: the stone is brown; the roof of red pantiles.*

Left: *The staircase of black marble with wrought-iron balusters supporting a steel handrail; the client had asked for an oak staircase – in vain.*

Above: *The sitting room in the south-west wing: perhaps the interiors of Heathcote lack the excitement of the exterior of this Italianate villa.*

On a new site, Lutyens created a three-storey symmetrical villa with a pantiled roof and flanking two-storey wings in which he played variations on the theme of the rusticated Doric order used by Sanmicheli on the Porta del Palio in Verona, built in 1524–27 – which he only knew from drawings and photographs (in his book on *The Architecture of the Renaissance in Italy* first published in 1896, W. J. Anderson had illustrated this gate as 'one of the most admired productions of this scarcely rivalled master'). The celebrated letter to Baker of 29 January 1911 in which Lutyens described how he had designed Heathcote has already been quoted: 'I wanted something persisting and dominating, with horizontal lines, to stratify the diarhetic conditions produced by the promiscuous villadom: in fact an architectural bismuth! To get domination I had to get a scale greater than the height of my rooms allowed, so unconsciously the San Michele invention repeated itself. That time-worn doric order – a lovely thing – I have the cheek to adopt. You can't copy it. To be right you have to take it and design it … . You cannot copy: you find if you do you are caught, a mess remains. It means hard labour, hard thinking, over every line in all three dimensions and in every joint; and no stone can be allowed to slide …'. The reference to 'bismuth' is puzzling, until it is appreciated that Ruskin compared the 'monstrous' ornament on

Sanmicheli's Palazzo Grimani in Venice to the crystalline form of this rare soft metal in *The Seven Lamps of Architecture*. David Crellin therefore observes that 'Lutyens's use of the term implies that the elaborate classicism of his design for Heathcote was intended to have a corrective effect on the other buildings around it through being "monstrous". It was, in its suburban Yorkshire context, deliberately foreign, inappropriate and even shocking.'[134]

Heathcote shows hard thinking and cleverness throughout. There is a pantiled roof to the cornice above the principal Doric order, which is sometimes expressed as rusticated pilasters disappearing into the masonry courses; there are concave sides to some windows and carefully cut flat-arched lintels above; there are bold rusticated quoins framing balconies and niches on the terrace facing the gardens; there are grand arched chimneys inspired by Vanbrugh more than Sanmicheli. 'It all looks so simple and easy,' observed Weaver, 'and is, in fact, so very difficult to do well. There are no graces in the materials, in the Guisely stone walls, with grey dressings from the Morley quarries.' Inside, on the non-axial plan, there are grand spaces and marble columns – and that marble staircase.

Hemingway really seems to have been pleased by what he got, and he allowed Lutyens to advise on the treatment of the interior. 'We have had such a day,' Lutyens reported to his wife in August 1908, '– plans, plans, house, house – 8.30 till now. Curtains, carpets, gardeners, electricians, door handles, carvers, and now I go to Leeds to see the furniture makers tomorrow.'[135] And, three years later, Lady Emily could write that she had asked friends near Ilkley 'if they knew Hemingway's house. "Know it" they said, "why it is the great sight of the neighbourhood. Even Americans come to see it" and they said how wise Hemingway was to have put himself *entirely* in your hands.'[136]

Above: *The south-east pool below the garden terrace and the dining-room wing.*

Right: *The south terrace with its balconies, rusticated piers and the steps descending to the gardens.*

SIXTEEN

CASTLE DROGO

Castle Drogo was the last castle to be built in Britain. It is not a real castle, of course, but a house in which Lutyens played with the idea of a castle, evolving a rectilinear style of horizontal battlemented architecture, sublimely abstract in its severity. Although built of massive walls of Devon granite, it is very different from Victorian castles by Anthony Salvin or Billy Burges, as it is not a fanciful essay in archaeology: the design may owe something to Norman Shaw's Flete nearby, but perhaps it is closest in spirit to the castles of Vanbrugh. True, there is a working portcullis to the front door, but, as Christopher Hussey observed, 'The ultimate justification of Drogo is that it does not pretend to be a castle. It is a castle, as a castle is built, of granite, on a mountain, in the twentieth century.'

Yet when it was commissioned by Julius Drewe in 1910, Lutyens would have preferred to design something more modest.

'Mr Drewe writes a nice and exciting letter,' he reported in August 1910, 'to go on with the drawings not more than £50,000 though and £10,000 for the garden. I suppose £60,000 sounds a lot to you but I don't know what it means. If I look at Westminster Abbey it is an absurd – trivial amount. If I look at a dear little old world two roomed cottage it merely looks a vast and unmanageable amount.

Only I do wish he didn't want a castle but just a delicious loveable house with plenty of good large rooms in it'[137]

– something like Ednaston Manor, perhaps. Lutyens visited Drewsteignton the following month: 'We went to the site and then Mr Drewe arrived with his three nice sons and Mrs Drewe who is a dear. He changed the site of the castle again, wisely I think ... . Drewe told me of his dream of a Commemorative Tower or Keep and this we planned and plotted and he was mighty pleased and proud ... . We got on famously ...'. Lutyens prepared the first designs while he was on a Union Castle steamship to South Africa to design the Johannesburg Art Gallery; work began in April 1911 – a year before he first went to India to plan New Delhi. In the event, Drogo took as long to build as Viceroy's House – and even then what was built is less than half of what was originally proposed.

On one level, the story of Drogo is absurd. Julius Drew was a clergyman's son who, in partnership with John Musker, founded the Home and Colonial Stores. At the age of thirty-three, he was able to retire from the firm, set up as a country gentleman and add an 'e' to his surname. His barrister brother managed to convince him that the family was descended from one Drogo, or Dru, who had come over with the Conqueror, whose descendant, Drogo de Teynton, had given his name to the parish of Drewsteignton on the edge of Exmoor where, as luck would have it, Mrs Drewe's cousin had been the rector. So Drewe bought 450 acres nearby, including a granite outcrop overlooking the River Teign which seemed the perfect site for a real castle. Edward Hudson then advised him who was 'the only possible architect'.

The evolution of the design of Castle Drogo was complicated and has been elucidated by Peter Inskip. The first designs envisaged a castle arranged around a courtyard, with the entrance to the north and a Great Hall to the south on the edge of the crag overlooking the river. By 1911 this had evolved into a more compact plan, with an open court facing north. In November 1911, Lutyens made the crucial decision to splay the sides of this courtyard outwards by moving the domestic and service wings through 20 degrees – it is this angle in the plan which adds to the picturesque drama of the spectacular fragment of Drogo that was built. One problem was that the brief was vague: 'The lack of certainty at Drogo meant that only visual requirements were left to predominate and the house could only depend on ideas about massing and movement through a sequence of spaces'.[138]

Drewe did, however, make one decision which would have far-reaching consequences. When he discovered that Lutyens proposed

a 2-foot cavity between two 2-foot-thick walls, Drewe insisted that his castle should have authentic 6-foot-thick granite walls. This was unfortunate for posterity in that the wind drives the rain through the joints to cause mischief inside. Furthermore, the increase in the estimated price to achieve these solid walls was considerable, and then Drewe began to realise that he did not need all the accommodation originally proposed. So, in October 1912, a reduced scheme was adopted which consisted of the eastern half of the house only. As far as Lutyens was concerned, this was not satisfactory. He tried to persuade Drewe to extend the northern wing with a screen and castellated gateway over the approach drive and, in the summer of 1913, a full-size timber mock-up of these was constructed: but in vain.

Then war came, and in July 1917, Julius Drewe's eldest son was killed at Ypres. His heart went out of the great project, but his two younger sons had survived the Western Front and persuaded him to see the thing through. The Great Hall was now abandoned and a chapel formed in its crypt with an apse and a bell-cote, while the south wing was redesigned. The last stone was placed on Castle Drogo in December 1925 and the giant crane that had hovered over it at last dismantled, but the house was not finished until 1930 – a year before the deaths of Julius Drewe and John Walker, the clerk of works and master mason, who had overseen the work almost from the beginning.

In some ways, the design benefited from this long building process. Although a fragment, Castle Drogo is superbly massed and composed, while Lutyens's castle style became more abstract, relying on the integrity of the planes of granite rather than on direct historical quotation. In 1912, Drewe was disconcerted to find that Lutyens had apparently altered his instructions as to the treatment of the walls. 'May I ask why you have altered your opinion as to the preparation of the granite facing? From the commencement you expressed your firm decision that only rough

Preceding pages (left): The extraordinary, intimidating south end of the incomplete castle, as redesigned after the First World War.
(right): The entrance and west front of Castle Drogo: what was originally intended to be only the western side of a much bigger castle.

Above: The staircase down to the dining room: while the steps descend, the ceiling remains level.

Right: Piranesian grandeur – the central staircase between the main block and the wing which contrives to accommodate several different floor levels.

granite should be used. You told Jenkin that no toolmarks were to be visible on any piece. He went on with what you had told him to do and would have gone on doing so had you been detained in Delhi. To my mind ... the building should be continued to your pre-Delhian instructions. What might have happened to us if you had also seen the Pyramids as well makes us quake to think about.' His architect then replied that 'the big lumpy blocks are right for the lower courses but quite impossible to carry them up ... it would mean a barbaric building worthy of a small municipal corporation. When a barbarian built a fortress he heaped up rocks and hid his women behind them. If those hard white stones are what you think I meant I am the Barbarian! I am very keen about your castle and must "fight" you when I *know* I am right.'[139]

Lutyens's castle style owed much to the simplified 'Tudor' of the Bristol Central Library by Charles Holden (for H. Percy Adams) – a remarkable building, published in 1906, which also had an influence on the west wing of Mackintosh's Glasgow School of Art. But Lutyens went further, assisted by his obsessive interest in maintaining the integrity of wall planes, as can be seen in the subtle recessive modelling of the entrance bay, ennobled by 'Mr Drewe's Lion'. Perhaps the most powerful and sculptural part of the castle is the south wing, as redesigned after the abandonment of the contiguous Great Hall. Severely simple mullioned and transomed windows light the dining room and the drawing room above. At basement level, the granite wall is sheer and unbroken, but then it is subtly stepped back with a chamfer as the building rises, leaving the windows as if in a projecting oriel bay and the corners reading as abstracted battlements, with razor-sharp 45-degree angles – adding, so A. S. G. Butler thought, 'a kind of diabolic malevolence'.[140]

Inside, the planning of Drogo may be unsatisfactory owing to the several changes of mind, but the spaces are magnificent – even in the service areas. The great kitchen in the basement of the north wing is covered by a top-lit dome reminiscent of the banking halls by John Soane in the Bank of England, which were being demolished in the 1920s by Lutyens's former friend Sir Herbert Baker. Best of all, perhaps, are monumental staircases contained within sheer granite walls, especially the central staircase, which accommodates the different floor levels between the main block and the angled wing beneath vaults and saucer domes of granite. It is architecture at a very high level of sophistication and imagination. As Peter Inskip has written, 'Even if Lutyens shared his client's fantasy by including sketches of Drogo de Teynton riding up to his castle in his preliminary perspectives, there is a determination to be serious manifest in the building.'[141]

The library on the ground floor, immediately beyond the entrance: a grand room looking east with, it would seem, no books in it.

Above: *The grandest of kitchens – covered by a dome like those inside
Soane's Bank of England which were being demolished when Castle Drogo
was nearing completion.*

Right: *Mr Drewe's own bathroom, in which he could contemplate
the nobility of the Doric order while soaking in his bath.*

Castle Drogo rises proudly on its rugged, dramatic site, with no gardening to soften the impact of the massive granite walls. Both client and architect wished to retain the wild and open approach from the north-east, so there are neither lodges nor entrance gates. But there is, in fact, a formal garden, designed by George Dillistone in collaboration with Lutyens and hidden behind the trees to the north of the house. The lower part has raised terraces flanking a rectangular garden, whose axis is projected eastwards up steps, which climb first to a rectangular lawn framed by retaining walls and yew hedges, and then yet higher to a huge circular lawn created by more yew hedges. If Lutyens responded to nature in the design of the castle, in the gardens he made hedges and trees perform as pure, abstract architecture.

Photographs of Castle Drogo were taken by A. E. Henson in 1929 but these were not published until A. S. G. Butler described the house in *Country Life* for 3 and 10 August 1945. The house was bequeathed to the National Trust in 1974, so becoming the first (complete) twentieth-century house to be opened to the public.

Left: *A distant view of the castle on its headland, seen from the north-west across the Devon countryside.*

Above: *Part of the formal gardens with concavities and convex projections along the edge of the path, making a pattern which Lutyens normally used as a joinery detail.*

SEVENTEEN

ABBEY HOUSE

Imperious and severe, Abbey House at Barrow-in-Furness is another essay in the abstracted, military Tudor style that Lutyens was evolving for Castle Drogo. Although not a castle itself, it is an unusual building and, despite appearances, not really a country house. Rather, it was built as a guesthouse for the heads of state and arms dealers visiting the nearby dockyard of Messrs Vickers, Sons & Maxim – at which, during that fraught decade of the 'Naval Race' with Germany which preceded the outbreak of the Great War, most of the Royal Navy's submarines were laid down.

Barrow-in-Furness is a strange and remote place. 'What might have been a northern Venice,' as Peter Fleetwood-Hesketh put it, 'warmed by the Gulf Stream and protected by the long breakwater of Walney Island, has grown instead, since the opening of the Furness Railway in 1846, from a small hamlet on a remote peninsula into a large place of docks, shipbuilding and other industries, founded on the great mineral resources of the district.'[142]

And the site for Abbey House was a bleak and windswept one, overlooking the magnificent ruins of Furness Abbey just outside the steel-manufacturing dockyard town. 'Eastward, blue and mysterious, rise the Lancashire fells,' to quote the overheated prose of Christopher Hussey in the first article he wrote on a building by Lutyens for *Country Life*, 'and to the west the sky is lit by the blast furnaces at night; while from the roof of the house can be seen by day monster cranes in ranks, raised up on their steel legs, in appearance like a company of Mr Wells' Martians.'

The commission came in 1913. Lutyens visited Barrow in April and wrote gloomily to his wife having seen what remained of the Abbey: 'And what avail is it to build at all when great buildings [after] a very few hundred years are in ruins in spite of their permanent methods of construction that is of no avail against destruction and neglect? Very depressing. I saw the site for the Vickers Maxim Entertainment House I am to build and then went over their great works and a great battle cruiser just completing for the Japanese. 13.5 guns and lots of them and a mass of men – English and a lot of Japs just arrived and amongst them a policeman whose appearance tickled me.'[143]

Abbey House was designed both as a home for the managing director of Vickers' Barrow works, Sir James McKechnie, and to provide accommodation for some occasional but rather grand visitors, like the King of Siam. 'In short,' wrote Hussey in that article published on 2 April 1921, 'on the one hand, a compact and homely residence was desired, and, on the other, something like a private hotel. It was a happy inspiration to adopt the H plan of a Tudor building, where the similar necessity of lodging for the lord and his family, with the certainty of numerous guests and retainers making periodical descents on the house, had caused the H plan to be evolved … . The Great Hall, with the private apartments at one end and the offices at the other, was an ideal and ready-made disposition for the Abbey House.' But no Elizabethan house is as

Preceding pages (left): A view of Abbey House from the east which emphasises the severity of the two projecting end bays facing the gardens.
(right): A distant view of the entrance front from the approach drive from the north; the house is built of red sandstone.

Left: The main entrance to the guesthouse, modest in scale, with, above, the arms of Messrs Vickers, Sons & Maxim and the fateful date of completion.

Below: The vestibule beyond the porch; the Great Hall lies behind the fireplace. The door to the left of that most compelling motif – a single Doric column – leads to a cloakroom; on the right is a cupboard.

severe and as precise as Lutyens's pile; absolutely symmetrical about the projecting entrance tower – even to the disposition of the tall chimneys, so reminiscent of the funnels on a contemporary battle cruiser – the house is characterised by the areas of plain stone walling and by the ruthlessly consistent horizontality of the parapet line.

Inside, the house was more welcoming, although the walls of the lateral vestibule are of hard ashlar stone. The Great Hall has a deep trabeated ceiling over the whole space, within which the disposition of oriel window, screen and staircase behind is similar to that at Little Thakeham, except that the detail is less Baroque and more abstract. The drawing room is covered by a grand Soanean dome; the dining room by a simple plaster barrel vault. The principal bedrooms are on the first floor, with more bedrooms placed in a mezzanine where the ground-floor arrangement of high and low rooms permitted it. The managing director's house was in one of the lower, outer wings, the kitchens in the other, and at the side of both the ground was lowered so that the basement is properly lit (a similar solution was adopted at Viceroy's House at about the same time).

Next to the company's coat of arms over the modest arched entrance is carved the ominous date of completion – 1914. Abbey House does not express the opulence of the Edwardian years; rather it seems in its treatment to anticipate the abstract severity of the war memorials Lutyens would design after the catastrophe of the First World War. The *Country Life* photographs cannot convey the colour of the red Cumbrian sandstone of which Abbey House is built, but Christopher Hussey was surely right when, some three decades after his pioneering article, he concluded that 'Rather grim and impersonal, as efficient as a battleship, the work caught something of the mood in which it was conceived'. In 1951, Abbey House was made into an old people's home and badly treated; in 1984, it was sold by Cumberland County Council and now functions, very appropriately, as a hotel.

Below: *The Great Hall, seen from the billiard room; the spatial arrangement with a screen and a staircase behind is similar to that in the hall at Little Thakeham.*

Right: *The drawing room, covered by a dome in plaster which might possibly have been inspired by the work of Sir John Soane.*

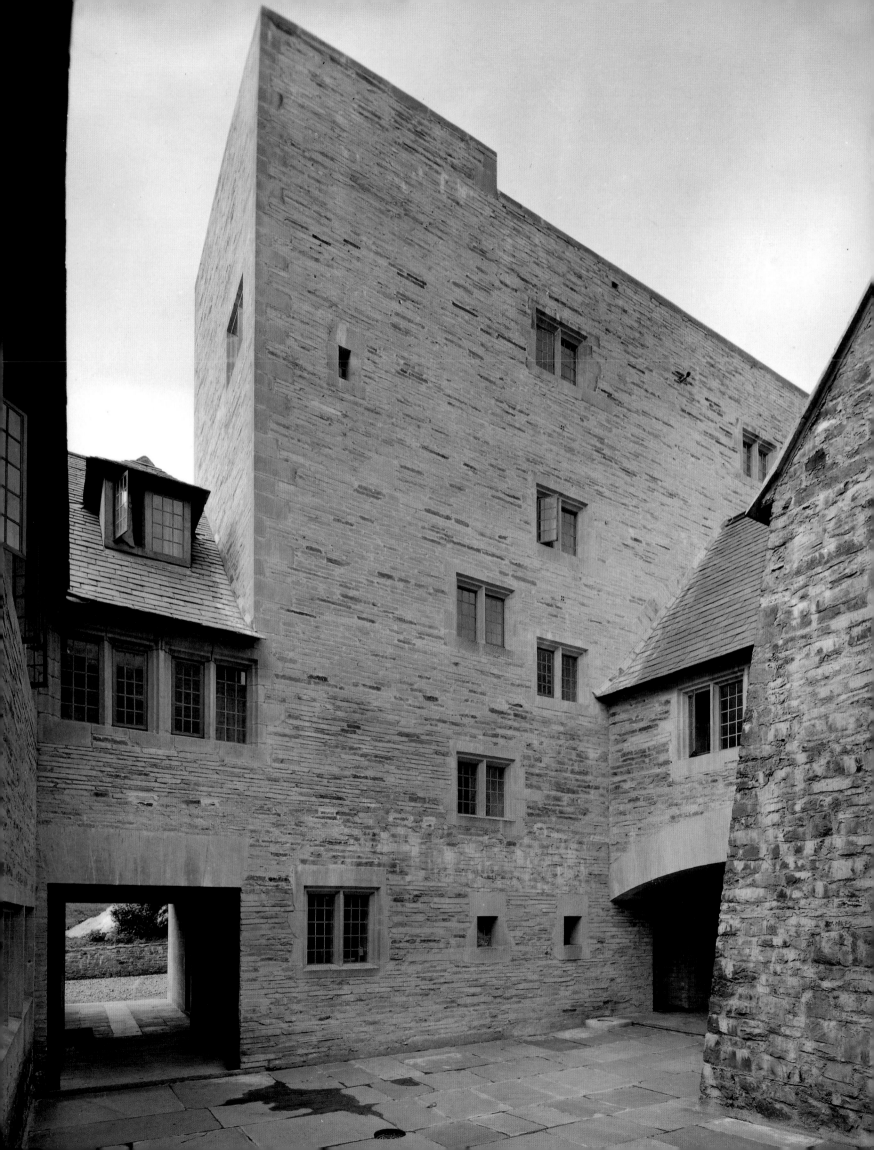

EIGHTEEN

PENHEALE MANOR

The addition Lutyens made to Penheale Manor in Cornwall just after the Great War is not well known, but it is a fine example of his ability to work sympathetically with old and historic buildings without being too much constrained by the self-denying philosophy preached by the Society for the Protection of Ancient Buildings. The new work follows naturally, almost seamlessly, from the old, but it is also distinct and interesting in itself. As Ralph Edwards put it when he wrote about the house for *Country Life* in 1925, 'To enlarge an old house by a meticulous imitation of its original features is to confess a belief that architecture is dead, and, paradoxical as it may seem, to be false to tradition'. The new wing at Penheale also demonstrates continuity with Lutyens's pre-war work, for he used the austere and abstracted castle style that he had evolved for Castle Drogo not far away in neighbouring Devon.

Penheale Manor at Egloskerry, near Launceston, is a rugged and complicated house, originally medieval, rebuilt by George Grenville in the late sixteenth century, and then extended in the reign of Charles I. It was 'almost ruinous' when it was bought by Captain Norman Robert Colville, M.C., who had been badly gassed in the trenches and had been advised to move south from Scotland for the sake of his health. Colville needed a home for his growing collection of works of art, for he was a connoisseur of Old Master drawings and of English furniture.

In 1920 he asked Lutyens to restore Penheale and to add a service wing and more bedrooms. A first design made was in a neo-Georgian manner, but, fortunately, this was superseded.

Lutyens's additions lie to the south of the second courtyard of the old house. At first, the roofline continues that of the older structure, but then pitched roofs and gables give way to a plain, stone tower, a sort of miniature Drogo – or another Red House, Godalming, if in blue-grey Polyphant stone rather than red brick. The walls rise up four storeys to a straight parapet, with no roof visible. At the side, however, this dramatic tower does not seem quite so tall and assertive, as the ground is higher and laid out as a rose garden approached by steps from a lower garden in front of the old house.

If to be modern is to be simple, with a flat roof, then this work at Penheale – like other designs by Lutyens of the time – is unashamedly modern. Even Nikolaus Pevsner was impressed. 'Its main accent is asymmetrical and very bold,' he wrote in the very first of his *Buildings of England* volumes to be published, 'a tower-like structure, sheer and flat. Yet it stands up perfectly to the old work, by virtue of its obstinate originality.'[144] And John Betjeman, in his Shell guide to the county, explained how well Lutyens had sited his extension: 'It is fine in itself and groups beautifully with the old house when seen from all sides except the main front of the old house from which it is cunningly designed to be invisible.'[145]

The other part of Lutyens's task was to repair the interior of the original manor. The best room is the Long Gallery, with its

Preceding pages (left): *The tower of Lutyens's new bedroom wing at Penheale Manor, seen from inside the courtyard beyond the old house.*
(right): *The new wing, seen from the south-east; the additional bedrooms are in the four-storey tower to the left.*

Above: *The sixteenth-century stone Tudor front of the original manor house seen from the old gatehouse loggia; Lutyens's extension lies beyond it to the right.*

Right: *The new wing seen from the west: the older parts of the house are to the left behind the raised rose garden.*

pendentive barrel plaster ceiling ornamented with heraldry and a bold pattern of snaking ribs. The presence of the Grenville crest shows that the design is sixteenth century, but, in truth, two-thirds of the room is modern. When Captain Colville bought Penheale Manor, there were three rooms here. In the course of his adaptation and restoration of the house, Lutyens cleverly knocked them into one, and continued the original plaster ceiling design by taking moulds of the old work. The result is a long room of great beauty in which the owner placed the cream of his collection of old English furniture.

Penheale Manor was photographed, inside and out, by Arthur Gill for *Country Life* and the results published on 28 March and 4 April 1925. In his book *Search for a Style: Country Life and Architecture, 1897–1935*, John Cornforth suggests that the fact that the accompanying articles were written by Ralph Edwards indicates how important collecting such furniture was considered at the time. He also observes that in some of the unpublished photographs, the furniture and works of art are in different positions, suggesting that Colville objected to certain objects being published and insisted on the views being taken again: 'Today the luxury of such changes of mind could not be afforded.'

Top: *Three storeys of Lutyens's bedroom tower seen from across the raised rose garden.*

Above: *The hall in the original manor house, with the timber Renaissance screen of c.1640.*

Right: *The gallery, with Captain Colville's collection of furniture: originally a sixteenth-century room but extended by Lutyens to occupy the whole length of the old manor house.*

NINETEEN

GLEDSTONE HALL

In his volume on *Country Houses* in the *Lutyens Memorial*, A. S. G. Butler described Gledstone Hall as 'a work of art worthy of being listed, one day, as a national monument'. It is, needless to say, now a listed building, but many may think that Gledstone is one of the houses by Lutyens less worthy of being preserved – certainly compared with his earlier, more romantic efforts. The house is elegant and very correct, but somehow cold and unloveable – and this is not because it lies by the Yorkshire Moors rather than in cosy Surrey. It displays less of the invention and imagination so evident in other houses – both Classical and vernacular – and seems somehow to express the conservatism and uncertainty of a Britain damaged and exhausted by the First World War. The exuberance of the Edwardian years has gone; at Gledstone, Lutyens seems to be playing by the rules rather than playing games, and the result has little of the inventive and purposeful abstraction found in his contemporary work for the Imperial War Graves Commission.

Preceding pages (left): *The loggias on the south front of Gledstone Hall facing the gardens: the window shutters give the house a Continental air.*
(right): *The Ionic entrance portico on the north front of the house: the lateral arched walls were inspired by Inigo Jones's St Paul's Church, Covent Garden.*

Above (left): *The main staircase with the (highly dangerous) alternating treads of black and white marble.*
(right): *The staircase landing with its imaginative metalwork patterns and the coved ceiling above painted black.*

Yet Gledstone Hall is a creation to be reckoned with. The client was Sir Amos Nelson, who had made his fortune from cotton mills in Skipton and Nelson, and had bought a country house by Carr of York near the Yorkshire–Lancashire border. At first he asked a local architect, Richard Jaques, of Nelson, Lancashire, to reconstruct the Georgian house, and then he suggested that his architect might care to collaborate with someone of greater experience, and – having seen Heathcote – Jaques suggested Lutyens. The eventual result was, as Christopher Hussey wrote, that 'Sir Amos got the kind of house he wanted, which Mr Jaques assures us is a Lutyens house, whilst Lutyens acknowledged that he adopted many of his collaborator's proposals'.

As with Castle Drogo, Lutyens prepared his first drawings for Gledstone Hall on the high seas. En route to Bombay on the SS *Caledonia*, he wrote to Lady Emily in December 1920 that 'I have been working on Gledstone Hall and the owner, a pleasant cotton spinner, is on board so I have to work to keep his interest to a pitch higher than the toss of waves'.[146] In the event, the cost of the proposed reconstruction reached a higher pitch than Nelson had

anticipated, so it was decided to build a new, smaller house on a slightly higher site. The plans were finally agreed in 1923 and the resulting 'little palace' completed three years later.

India might seem to have had an influence on Gledstone; the axial planning of both house and gardens is reminiscent of the formality of Viceroy's House. The external envelope of the house is symmetrical and the approach from the north to the portico is between two flanking lodges. On the garden side, a long sunken garden between retaining walls, with a reflecting pool down the centre, stretches away to the south (the gardens were planted to the advice of the aged Gertrude Jekyll). The Ionic entrance portico, its flanking walls pierced by arches, is of the type derived from Inigo Jones's church in Covent Garden which Lutyens had already used on the Johannesburg Art Gallery. On either side, the walls of local sandstone are penetrated by tall, thin windows. On the slightly projecting wings, these windows are asymmetrically placed as if in response to convenience, but, on the whole, Lutyens's ordered fenestration – with the larger, upper windows suggesting a non-existent *piano nobile* – bears no relation to internal arrangements.

On the garden elevation, the pediment alone is repeated – quite gratuitously – and there are twin loggias with Roman Doric columns. But what dominates is the overall roof of graded Gloucestershire slates, entirely unbroken by dormers and pitched at

Right: *The vaulted ground-floor corridor with its floor of black and white marble laid to an unusual pattern full of movement.*

Top: *The south front, seen from the end of the formal garden with its
long canal and circular terminating pool.*

Above: *Looking south from the house down the sunken
formal garden.*

The southern end of the formal garden, with steps and pergolas flanking the pool and overlooking a view of the Yorkshire Moors.

Lutyens's ideal steep angle of 54.45 degrees (the roofs are at a lower pitch on the lodges). This roof, together with the tall windows and the overall horizontality, brings, as Hussey put it, 'something of the France of Louis XVI into Yorkshire'.

Inside the house, Lutyens (or Jaques?) abandoned the usual intriguing complexity of plan, for this is the only significant Lutyens house (other than Deanery Garden, where the plan and intention are quite different) in which the symmetry is obvious and it is possible to walk in a straight line through the entrance, across the hall and out into the garden; it is also the only house with a conventional Classical portico – perhaps the legacy of Carr of York overawed him. The drawing room lies on one side of this central axis, the dining room and staircase on the other. There is certainly invention and subtlety at Gledstone: the external walls are laid on a batter and, inside, the staircase is a thrilling essay in geometry under a black coved ceiling. It was here that Lutyens played his games. The marble treads are alternately black and white (and thus dangerous to use), with some of the black treads being extended laterally: one to become the dado rail on the ground floor, another to be the level of the first floor and then projected around the walls

to become the sill of the windows. Otherwise, the corridors seem more interesting spaces than the reception rooms.

In considering the legacy of Lutyens, Gledstone Hall would seem to be a test for taste. For Christopher Hussey – who first wrote up the house in *Country Life* for 13 and 20 April 1935 with photographs by A. E. Henson – 'It is the conception of the English country house, as an art form, raised to its highest pitch, and thus ministering to the spirit rather than to the body'. But for Roderick Gradidge, 'it is a cold house and it makes an unhappy end to the housebuilding career of one of the greatest house designers that the world has ever known'.[147] There is much to admire – not least the apparent grand scale given to a comparatively small country house (only seven bedrooms) – yet if the house still seems pedestrian, it is certainly not because it is Classical rather than Tudor or vernacular but because it lacks the Mannerist fireworks of Heathcote and the truly original development of the Classical language displayed at Viceroy's House. Even so, Sir Amos got what he wanted.

167

TWENTY

PLUMPTON PLACE

Plumpton Place was the third and last of the country houses (or weekend retreats) that Lutyens designed or altered for his great patron
and friend, Edward Hudson. At Sonning on the Thames, he had created a modern evocation of Tudor romance;
at Lindisfarne, off the coast of Northumberland, he had enhanced a most romantic castle; now, in East Sussex, he repaired, enlarged
and ennobled an old tile-hung, timber-framed manor house, making it a dream of loveliness in a beautiful garden.
In a way, Lutyens was returning here both to his own roots and to the original conception of *Country Life Illustrated* – the celebration of
traditional English domestic architecture and the associated gardens. For Nikolaus Pevsner, writing in the 1960s,
Plumpton was 'an enchanted place due to Lutyens and rare birds'.[148]

In 1928, Hudson bought the derelict, moated manor house and naturally asked Lutyens how to deal with the house and its surroundings. Following the architect's advice, the lakes were then cleared, new cascades were installed, the gardens laid out with paths and intricate steps, and new cottages and a bridge built. It was fitting that one of Lutyens's late designs should have been for a landscape, as he had designed gardens throughout his career and his compositions of steps, terraces, walls, pergolas and pools were integral to his conception of a house in the country. What, however, was sad was that Gertrude Jekyll was now too old and frail to work with her protégé on creating this new garden for Hudson – she died in 1932. After all, it had been Miss Jekyll who had introduced Lutyens to Hudson and they had worked together on the superb garden at Deanery Garden; she had also been involved at Lindisfarne Castle.

Above: *The rustic bridge designed by Lutyens to connect the old manor house with his new gatehouse: the oak structure is cantilevered out from brick arches.*

Right: *Some of the new steps planned by Lutyens, leading from the lake up to the side of the old manor house.*

Preceding pages (left): *The new steps and terraces in the gardens around the lakes at Plumpton Place, dredged and restored by Edward Hudson.*
(right): *The new music room added to the old manor house by Lutyens in 1933–34, seen from across the lake.*

Above: *The inner, rose-garden side of the cottages forming the new gatehouse with its central passage in the form of a Palladian window.*

Oddly enough, Hudson never lived in Plumpton Place itself, and he left the restoration of the old house, with its many gables, great chimneys and massive roof with banks of dormers, until last – until shortly before he died, in 1936. He preferred to use the old weather-boarded Mill House at the end of the lower lake which Lutyens had restored for him. Hudson stayed in this house at weekends to superintend the making of the gardens. 'The rooms in the Mill House were charmingly furnished with simple but highly desirable eighteenth-century furniture,' John Cornforth has recorded, 'and suggest how Hudson's own taste had continued to move forward, in the process confirming the impression of the excellence of his eye.'[149]

Lutyens clearly enjoyed himself at Plumpton. In terms of architecture rather than landscape gardening, the dominant aspect of the work carried out immediately after 1928 is the new approach to the old house across the moat. New cottages were grouped together to form a gatehouse, from which a path leads over an enchanting bridge, a structure of oak corbelled and cantilevered out from a thin wall of brick, pierced by two arches to take it over the water. This gatehouse demonstrates that, despite his current preoccupations with grand Classical banks and reorganising London with new bridges across the Thames, he had not lost his feeling for the sweet vernacular of the South of England.

This symmetrical group is weather-boarded and dominated by a sweeping roof topped by tall brick chimneys. Each side is different, and the ground-floor windows only look outwards, while the upper-floor windows only look inwards, towards the manor house. At the ends of the wings, which point inwards, and below the little gambrel gables at the ridge, the slope of the hipped gable comes down, barn-like, almost to the ground. Dormer windows poke up from the eaves and, in the centre, pull up the roofline over an Ionic Palladian arch. Just as in some of his earliest buildings, the vernacular and the Classical are effortlessly and wittily combined.

Lutyens also designed 'a large music room, or gallery' as an extension to Plumpton Place itself, but when the gardens were described by Christopher Hussey in *Country Life* for 20 May 1933,

the planned restoration and enlargement of the old house had yet to be carried out. The photographs had been taken by A. E. Henson in 1930, but when the photographer returned four years later he was able to record the new structure. It is an abstracted essay in the Home Counties vernacular, a rectilinear structure rising from the lakeside above a stone base, with tile-hung walls and a pair of great timber-framed oriel windows below a tiled roof, all blending effortlessly with the fabric of the old house behind.

But the new music room is also a remarkable composition in itself, upright, angular and symmetrical, with the grid of the timber windows wrapping around the corners and giving the lakeside façade that intriguing duality that Lutyens clearly liked. Perhaps those oriels, for the aged Hudson, were a reminiscence of the hall at Deanery Garden (where the top tier of lights was also continued laterally). But on the inside, the rectilinear grid of timber set against plain white plaster, with the window placed at the corner, seems as abstract and as modern as the treatment of any contemporary 'Functionalist' house of the 1930s. The glazing may be of small leaded panes set into oak rather than sheets of plate glass framed in steel, but the architectural intention is surely similar.

If the critics who still dismiss Lutyens as backward-looking could see beyond the tile-hanging and the Classical columns, they might comprehend that his architecture is as much a part of the twentieth century as that of Mackintosh or Wright; indeed, in his grasp of pure architecture, in his handling of space and of form, he could be as 'modern' – to use a word so overworked as to become almost meaningless – as Mies van der Rohe or Le Corbusier, and rather more versatile. But, on the other hand, the plain fact is that oak and lime plaster are more comfortable to live with than steel and reinforced concrete. 'How to express enjoyment can but lie within the hearts of those whose joy lies within their Craft,' Lutyens said at the time he was working at Plumpton. 'There is wit and may be humour in the use of materials. The unexpected, where it is logical, is fun. The time may come when we shall be able to choose girders to our taste, as we select the particular boughs of particular Oaks for struts and braces. Then will girders become friendly and personal and not mere reach-me-downs sold by the pound, with a have-me-or-not attitude, the noise of their rolling giving no reprieve.'[150]

But that time has still not yet come …

Left: *Functionalism in oak – one of the oriel-window bays in the unfurnished interior of the new music room designed by Lutyens.*

Above: *The interior of the old manor house after the restoration by Lutyens carried out after 1933: the panelling is old, the floor clearly new.*

TWENTY-ONE

MIDDLETON PARK

Middleton Park was Lutyens's last house and the only country house that Lutyens built for a member of the old landed aristocracy.
Not that it is a pure Lutyens house; rather it is Double Lutyens, for he designed it in collaboration with his only son, Robert.
The client was the 9th Earl of Jersey, who, as well as owning Osterley, had a seat at Middleton Stoney in Oxfordshire. This had been rebuilt in 1755 and altered in the nineteenth century. In 1932, soon after he came of age, the young Lord Jersey closed the house, and he demolished it two years later. For the new and luxurious house he proposed instead, he approached Robert Lutyens, but Edward Hudson advised him to consult his father as well. This was a happy experience for both, as it confirmed a reconciliation after some years of estrangement. Robert Lutyens (1901–72) had even less formal training as an architect than his father and never passed an examination.
Having briefly served in the army as a cook, he had gone up to Cambridge, where, according to his sister, Mary,
'He does not seem to have learned anything … except how to make *crème brûlée*'.[151] He then made what was – in his father's eyes –
a most unsuitable marriage. Then, after a time as a journalist – starting at *Country Life* – Robert Lutyens began to work as an interior decorator and entered into partnership with one of his father's former assistants, Harold Greenwood.

As to the relative responsibilities of father and son at Middleton Park, the latter put the record straight in 1959: 'Lutyens's biographers have said that Middleton was a "collaboration and one of special interest because Lutyens entered into partnership with his son … . It was their joint responsibility; and we are told that the arrangement gave Sir Edwin great pleasure in that it fulfilled his hopes." This is not precisely the case. The son's object was much simpler than that. While acting professionally as a sympathetic mediator between disparate generations, nevertheless his chief desire, and one which was amply fulfilled, was to stand sufficiently close to his father to be able to watch him actually at work. The work that mattered was all the father's.' And Robert Lutyens considered that, 'At Middleton especially Lutyens reduced the classical modes of antiquity to a quintessential Englishness which embodied the total experience of his life.'[152]

This house has similarities with Gledstone, but it is less pretentious and more inventive within the formal constraints. There is no portico, but an elaborate rusticated door set in the centre of a screen wall of beautiful Clipsham stone. The design shows Lutyens's Ruskinian obsession with the integrity of the wall plane, as well as with the continuity of horizontals. Subsidiary doors set in subtle recesses have Gibbs surround quoins flush with the dominant wall plane – a plane which is also that of the subtly projecting wings. The wall then continues to link up with the group of four lodges – each with a high-pitched roof and a central chimney – which guard the entrance. Lutyens intended that these should be balanced by a projection of the wall and a gateway to enclose the forecourt at the west, but this was never carried out.

Middleton Park has similar tall, thin windows to Gledstone, and the French feel is enhanced by the presence of shutters. But the building Middleton most resembles is that masterpiece of under-stated authority, Kinross House in Scotland. There is not only the same disposition of windows and similar upright massing, with the three-bay ends breaking slightly forward, but also the adoption of an unusual attic strip (pierced by small square windows) between the principal cornice and the eaves of the dominating hipped roof, topped by prominent chimneys. In designing Kinross in the late seventeenth century, however, Sir William Bruce did not have to deal with the functional and technological constraints imposed on Sir Edwin Lutyens. As Christopher Hussey wrote about Middleton Park, 'Technically it is interesting as demonstrating how the

luxurious requirements of the time – a dozen bathrooms, with accommodation for numerous visiting valets and maids – could be met within the framework of the aesthetic science without water-pipe or a window conflicting with the symmetrical unity.'

Inside, the house is ingeniously planned for living and entertaining, without the simplistic axial symmetry of Gledstone. The central axis of the grand, vaulted entrance vestibule is broken by the back wall of the drawing-room chimney, necessitating a journey along the lateral corridor, across the staircase hall with its Delhi Order of columns, then through the smoking room and two more right-angled turns before the drawing room is reached. This is another house where the circulation spaces seem more interesting than the reception rooms, and the service stair more elegant than the main staircase.

And then there were those fourteen bathrooms. Although A. S. G. Butler lamented that 'only three of them have the ordinary bath which the Englishman expects', all was redeemed by Lady Jersey's own bathroom, once the glory of the house. The second Lady Jersey was the former American actress Virginia Cherrill, whose own first (brief) marriage had been to Cary Grant. She certainly understood plumbing. In the words of Christopher Hussey in writing up Middleton Park in *Country Life* for 5 and 12 July 1946 (with photographs by A. E. Henson), her bathroom was 'a notable instance of the between-wars cult of the tub. With a barrell and cross vaulted ceiling, its walls are of pink onyx and white marble, the metalwork is gilt bronze. The shower occupying the innermost section is enclosed in purdah glass which presents a reflecting surface outside but is transparent from within.' This was, presumably, the work of Lutyens *fils* rather than *père*.

Middleton Park was completed in 1938, just before the Second World War. Lord Jersey did not move back into it after the war; the house was sold and subsequently divided into several flats.

Preceding pages (left): *The new Middleton Park seen from the gates between the entrance lodges: the guardian eagles were carved by William Reid Dick.* (right): *The south front of the rebuilt mansion, facing the gardens; the small square windows in the narrow attic are at floor level in the nurseries behind.*

Above: *The main staircase, constructed of teak; the columns supporting the upper floor are of Lutyens's Delhi Order.*

Right: *The vaulted entrance vestibule, looking outwards through the front door to the enclosed forecourt.*